W9-CAJ-553

THE HUNTING & FISHING LIBRARY®

The Complete Hunter™

DUCK HUNTING

By Dick Sternberg & Jeff Simpson

DICK STERNBERG has been an avid waterfowler since his high-school days. He enjoys any kind of duck hunting, but his favorite is hunting puddlers over a small decoy spread in a pothole, along with his two black labs, Nicky and Dixie.

JEFF SIMPSON, a fifth-generation waterfowl hunter, grew up hunting ducks on the prairie of South Dakota. He has hunted ducks from the northern grain fields of Saskatchewan to the bayous of Louisiana. An accomplished writer, he has authored many articles on a wide variety of outdoor topics.

COWLES
Creative Publishing, Inc.

President/COO: Nino Tarantino
Executive V.P./Editor-in-Chief: William B. Jones

DUCK HUNTING
By Dick Sternberg & Jeff Simpson

Executive Editor, Outdoor Products Group: Don Oster
Project Leaders: Mike Hehner, Jeff Simpson
Managing Editor: Denise Bornhausen
Copy Editor: Janice Cauley
Associate Creative Director: Brad Springer
Art Director: Dave Schelitzche
Senior Desktop Publishing Specialist: Joe Fahey
Desktop Publishing Specialist: Laurie Kristensen
V.P. Photography and Production: Jim Bindas
Studio Manager: Marcia Chambers
Studio Services Coordinator: Cheryl Neisen
Principal Photographer: William Lindner
Staff Photographers: Mike Hehner, Mark Macemon
Photo Assistants: Dan Carey, Thomas Heck, Dave Maas, Andria Moldzio, Frederick Strobel, David L. Tieszen, Ingrid Worthman
Production Manager: Kim Gerber
Production Staff: Dave Austad, Curt Ellering, Laura Hokkanen, Rob Johnstone, Phil Juntti, Kay Wethern
Digital Imaging: Brad Palm
Contributing Photographers: Aigrette Photography, Cliff Beittel, Blackhawk Productions, Denver Bryan, Bruce Crist, Dembinsky Photo Associates, Jeanne Drake, Ducks Unlimited – Matt Young, FRS Photography, Mike Gnatowski, The Green Agency, Cathy & Gordon Illg, Mark Kayser, Gary Kramer, Lance Krueger, Tim Leary, Gerry Lemmo, Stephanie McCloskey, Bill Marchel, Maslowski Wildlife, Margaret Thompson Mathewson, Minden Pictures, Neal Mishler, Scott Nielsen, Rich Images, Dick Simpson, Dale Spartas, Ron Spomer, Texas Inprint, VIREO, Keith Walters, The Wildlife Collection, Wildlife Research Photography, Gary Zahm

Contributing Manufacturers: Action Decoys – Bruce Barber; Alumacraft Boats – Jim Hobson; Backland Ltd. – Scott Anderson; Browning – Paul Thompson; Cabela's, Inc. – Stephanie Geiger; Carlson Championship Calls – Wendell Carlson; Carry-Lite Decoys, Inc. – Bob Kufaul; Columbia Sportswear – Tom Miller; Duck Commander Company; Federal Cartridge Company – Bill Stevens; Flagman Products – Randy Bartz; Flambeau Products Corp. – Mark Smith; Force Fin – Bob Evans; Haas Outdoors – Tack Robinson; Haydel's Game Calls, Inc. – Kelly Haydel; Herters – Pete Thiry; Hobie Outback – Bill Horner; I.W.S. – James Rollman; Kobuk; Lohman Calls – Brad Harris; Lowrance Electronics – Chad Warford; Mallard Master – Frank Bryant; Mossy Oak – Pam Reece; Muckworks Corporation – John Clark; Outlaw Decoys; Rich-N-Tone Products – Joel Benson, Buck Gardner; Riverside Products, Inc. – David Reed, Shawn Spakes; Sterns Manufacturing Company – Glenn Cook; Top Line Manufacturing – John Duncan; The W. C. Russell Moccasin Co. – Ralph Farbicius; Woods Calls Inc. – Ron Wieneke

Contributing Individuals and Agencies: Arkansas Dept. of Tourism – Richard Davies; Don Berger; Bayou Meto (AR) Public Hunting Area – Tim Moser; Bart Biedinger; Johnie Candle; John Cooper; Bruce "Wicker Bill" Crist; Delta Marsh Waterfowl – Lloyd Jones; Devils Lake (ND) State Park – Dick Horner; Duane Smith's Canvas Works; Ducks Unlimited – Chris Dorsey, George Horton; Rob Evans; Ferguson Keller Associates – Stu Wickland; Paul Flath; Tom Fogel; John Green; Hiedelbouer Calls – Frank Hiedelbouer; Indian Hills Resort – Kelly & Tolly Holtan; Skip James; Dr. Chris Johnson; Tim Larson; Mark LeJuine; Hal McMillin; Mickey McMillin; Ed Migale; North Dakota Game & Fish Dept. – Lynn Schuleter; North Dakota Tourism – Dawn Charging; Doug O'Connell; Tim Ohmann; 1,000 Island Waterfowl Specialist – Jim Costello; Dave Perkins; Prairie Land Outfitters – Don Anderson; Saskatchewan Dept. of Tourism – Gerard Mackusch; Dick Simpson; Robert Sloan; Spencer Vaa; Joel Vance; Vermont Waterfowl Guide Service – Tom Venezia

Printing: R. R. Donnelley & Sons Co.
00 99 98 97 / 5 4 3 2 1

Copyright © 1997 by Cowles Creative Publishing, Inc.
Formerly Cy DeCosse Incorporated
5900 Green Oak Drive
Minnetonka, Minnesota 55343
1-800-328-3895

Library of Congress Cataloging-in-Publication Data
Sternberg, Dick.
    Duck hunting / by Dick Sternberg & Jeff Simpson.
        p. cm. - - (The hunting & fishing library)
    Includes index.
    ISBN 0-86573-065-2 (hc)
    1. Duck hunting. 2. Ducks. I. Simpson, Jeff. II. Title.
SK333.D8S73 1997   III. Series.
799.2'44'097--dc21
                                          97-3676

Table of Contents

Introduction

To an avid duck hunter, the sound of wings whistling over a marsh on a gloomy November day is pure music. But, as a result of the lengthy drought that hit North America's duck factories in the 1980s and early 1990s, the music nearly stopped. Tired of looking at empty skies, many lifelong waterfowlers found better things to do with their time.

In only a few years, however, the morale of the nation's duck hunters took a dramatic turn for the better. When the drought finally broke, duck popula-

tions rebounded to levels beyond the dreams of even the most optimistic waterfowl biologists.

In addition to improved water conditions, a combination of factors have helped fuel the sensational comeback. The Conservation Reserve Program (CRP), which began in 1985, has provided millions of acres of grassland that ducks use for nesting cover. The mandatory use of steel shot has reduced the incidence of lead poisoning among waterfowl. And the protection of vital wetlands by conservation organizations, both public and private, has ensured that ducks will always have quality breeding habitat.

Even before the duck downturn, very few how-to duck-hunting books were written. Most authors focused on the rich tradition and romance of the sport. When it became apparent that duck hunting was on the decline, few books appeared on any duck-related topic. Consequently, beginning waterfowlers are

starving for solid how-to information and veterans have not learned of new innovations.

This book, entitled simply *Duck Hunting*, is intended to bring the sport into the twenty-first century. In order to be a successful duck hunter, you must first have a decent grasp of duck biology. This book shows you how to recognize good duck habitat and understand the birds' breeding behavior, food habits and migration patterns. It also includes biological profiles and excellent color photographs of every important North American duck species, both hen and drake.

Duck hunting is an equipment-intensive sport. This book will tell you what you need in the way of shotguns and shells, decoys, duck calls, blinds, boats, clothing, accessories and even hunting dogs. Then, we'll thoroughly explain how to put this equipment to the best use.

The highlight of the book is the section on duck-hunting techniques. Unlike any other duck-hunting book available, this one shows you exactly what to do in a wide variety of specific situations, from hunting puddle ducks on potholes to divers on big water. We explain how to scout for a good hunting spot, how to set your decoys and place your blind according to the wind and what guns and ammunition to use. We also give you some technique- and equipment-oriented tips that are sure to make your hunt more enjoyable and successful.

As long as we have an abundance of water and good nesting cover, duck populations should continue to flourish. So no matter if you're a newcomer anxious to enjoy some exciting wingshooting, a veteran waterfowler who gave up the sport or a diehard who stuck with it, use this book as your guide to the new world of duck hunting.

Understanding Ducks

Understanding Ducks

For centuries, ducks have been a source of fascination for hunters and nonhunters alike. But with so many duck species, learning to identify them and understand their behavior is a challenge, even to those who have spent a lifetime studying them.

Despite the inherent difficulty, duck hunters need to learn basic duck identification (pp. 16-47). Modern hunting regulations often distinguish between species and sometimes between sexes of the same species – not only in hand, but in the air. You may have a limit of five ducks, for instance, but only three of them can be mallards and, of those three, only one can be a hen. Some species, such as canvasbacks, may not be legal game in certain areas.

A complete duck identification guide, including wing charts, is beyond the scope of this book. For that information, refer to *North American Game Birds,* another volume in The Hunting & Fishing Library® book series.

A basic understanding of duck biology will also improve your hunting success. Knowledge of a bird's habitat preferences, food habits and migration timetable, for instance, is of obvious benefit in putting yourself in the right place at the right time.

Detailed range maps, found throughout this book, show you exactly where to find each species. You'll see where they breed and spend the summer, and where they winter. A color key for the range maps is shown at right.

Key to Duck Range Maps

breeding range

breeding & wintering range

wintering range

Duck Habitat

Although ducks can survive in a wide variety of habitats, they have one universal need: water. The habitat requirements of different kinds of ducks are summarized in the species accounts on pages 18 to 47.

Long-term droughts that dry up potholes and shrink other bodies of water pose a major threat to duck populations. During the 1980s, for example, a prolonged drought in the prairie pothole region reduced duck populations by about 50 percent. Another serious threat is wetland drainage.

Shown on this page are examples of the most common types of duck habitat.

PRAIRIE POTHOLES. The prairie pothole region, extending from South Dakota northward to the forests of Saskatchewan and Alberta, is North America's biggest "duck factory." The 1000-mile-long by 300-mile-wide zone (blue area on map) contains hundreds of thousands of potholes that periodically go dry.

TUNDRA WETLANDS. Lakes, marshes and meadows on tundra areas in the Far North provide an excellent breeding area for ducks, producing millions annually.

RIVER BACKWATERS. Marshes and sloughs connected to rivers produce more ducks than the rivers themselves. The fertile slack-water areas have lush weed growth.

BAYS OF LARGE LAKES. Shallow bays of natural and man-made lakes offer protection from the wind and a good supply of food, such as aquatic plants and invertebrates.

COASTAL WETLANDS. Estuaries in coastal areas provide a maze of bays, harbors and river mouths that make good wintering habitat for a wide variety of ducks.

MOUNTAIN WETLANDS. Valleys between mountain ranges often have large wetland areas that furnish the only duck habitat in that geographical region.

FOREST WETLANDS. Marshes, bogs and wooded swamps in forested areas make good habitat for many duck species, including wood ducks, black ducks, ringnecks and goldeneyes.

Pintail drakes chasing hen in courtship flight

Breeding

Most ducks are prolific breeders, capable of rapidly increasing their numbers when conditions are right. But when conditions are wrong, their numbers decline just as rapidly.

The prairie pothole region (p. 9) is the major duck-breeding zone in North America. When water levels in this region began to drop in the late 1970s, populations of most duck species began a long-term decline. When water levels were restored in the mid-1990s, however, duck populations rebounded accordingly. Contributing to the increase was the establishment of the Conservation Reserve Program, in which millions of acres of grasslands became available as nesting habitat. These unbroken expanses of grassland provide protection from predators.

Although breeding habits vary somewhat depending on the species of duck, there are many similarities:

•Most ducks select a mate and begin pair bonding by 6 months of age. Courtship flights (above) often determine which drake breeds with the hen. Puddle ducks usually breed in their first year, but many divers, such as canvasbacks, redheads and lesser scaup, don't breed successfully until their second year.

•Ducks do not necessarily mate for life, as geese generally do.

•Ducks usually copulate on the water.

Prime Duck-nesting Cover

PRAIRIE GRASS. Unbroken expanses of grassland near water make good nesting cover.

TUNDRA GRASS. This short grass makes adequate cover for ducks nesting on the tundra, where predators are scarce.

WETLAND FRINGES. Thick weedy or brushy cover bordering wetlands offers a secure nesting site.

•Depending on the species, ducks may nest on high ground, on wet ground near water, on mats of floating vegetation or even in tree holes. Some, such as ruddy ducks and redheads, may lay their eggs in the nest of another duck.

•The hen lays from 3 to 12 eggs, usually at a rate of 1 per day.

Mallard nest and eggs cushioned in down

•As the clutch nears completion, the hen lines the nest with feathers plucked from her own breast. The feathers serve as insulation and camouflage for the eggs when the hen leaves.

•Hens do not start to incubate the eggs until after the last one has been laid. In the interim, the eggs are subject to predation.

•If the first nesting attempt is not successful, ducks will often nest again, but broods are usually smaller.

•During incubation, many hens are killed by predators, explaining why the sex ratio in most duck species is skewed toward drakes.

•Drakes of most ducks do little to protect the nest and may never see their own offspring.

•As hatching time nears, the young begin *pipping,* pecking at the egg shell with their egg tooth. The entire clutch usually hatches in 5 to 6 hours.

•After hatching, the chicks *imprint* to the first moving object they see. In most cases, that object is a hen, but they have been known to imprint on a human or even a vehicle or piece of farm machinery.

•Most ducklings *fledge,* or learn to fly, at an age of 40 to 60 days, depending on species and geographic location. The farther north, the shorter the time to fledging.

Because of the prolific breeding habits of most ducks, waterfowl biologists now believe that regulations should allow hunters to take more birds when populations are high. Studies have shown that low bag limits will not "stockpile" ducks to ensure high populations in future years. Populations are more dependent on springtime water levels and undisturbed grassland cover than on fall hunting pressure.

Hen mallard and chicks

TREE HOLES. Old woodpecker holes or other tree holes are used for nesting by mergansers (above), wood ducks, goldeneyes and buffleheads.

MAN-MADE MALLARD NEST. These devices provide overhead cover and, because they're set on a pole in open water, keep out predators.

MAN-MADE NEST BOXES. Intended primarily for wood ducks, these boxes are occasionally used by other cavity-nesting ducks.

Shovelers use the lamellae on their bill (inset) to strain the water for food particles

Food Habits

Duck hunters who understand the food habits of their quarry should have no trouble finding good hunting spots. Even if it's impossible to hunt in an area where the birds are feeding, you may be able to intercept them as they fly between feeding and resting areas.

A summary of the food habits of each kind of duck is included in the species accounts on pages 18 to 47. For more detailed food-habit information, refer to *Ducks, Geese and Swans of North America,* by Frank C. Bellrose.

Some ducks, such as mallards, feed on a wide range of plant life, including both natural and cultivated types. They feed on the water or on land. Besides dozens of kinds of aquatic plants and their seeds, acorns and a variety of small grains, they will eat small animals, such as clams and snails. Because they can adapt to so many different kinds of foods, they can live most anywhere.

Other ducks are much more rigid in their feeding habits. The king eider, for example, feeds almost

A heavy bill helps sea ducks dislodge clams and snails

exclusively in deep water, often diving to depths of more than 100 feet to find clams, crabs and other aquatic invertebrates. This specialized mode of feeding explains why its range is limited to coastal areas.

Ducks that feed on plant seeds or small grains need grit in order for their gizzard to grind the food. When searching for grit on sand-gravel bottoms, they often ingest spent lead shot, resulting in lead poisoning. Ducks also ingest lead shot accidentally while feeding on aquatic plants or invertebrates. The lead-poisoning problem has resulted in a ban on the use of lead shot for waterfowl hunting throughout most of North America.

You can tell a great deal about the food habits of a particular kind of duck by closely examining its bill, as the photos on this page show.

A serrated bill (inset) helps mergansers hold onto fish

Molting

Even experienced waterfowlers may have difficulty identifying ducks in early season. Juvenile birds have not yet developed their adult plumage, and adult birds have not completed the *molt*, the process in which ducks annually shed and regrow their feathers.

The dull-colored feathers, or *eclipse plumage,* displayed by ducks that have not completed the molt can make it very difficult to distinguish between the sexes.

Drakes begin to molt soon after breeding, but molting in hens is delayed until the young are almost fully grown but have not developed the feathers necessary for flight.

Because the adults lose their primary feathers during the molt, they cannot fly for up to 2 months. They become very secretive during this period, hiding in cover where they won't be seen by predators. The molt usually takes place on certain large marshes that have become traditional molting areas.

By the latter part of the hunting season, most ducks have developed their full breeding plumage, which will carry into the next breeding season. At this point, identification becomes much easier.

Stages of the Molt (drake mallard)

MIDSUMMER (full eclipse). Drake resembles hen, except for greenish bill.

EARLY FALL (partial eclipse). Typical colors begin to develop.

LATE FALL (emerging). The coloration is almost fully developed.

WINTER (breeding plumage). The coloration is fully developed.

Migration

If you've ever witnessed a *grand passage* of water-fowl, you can understand why it's considered one of the most magnificent sights in all of nature. Spurred by the threat of an impending late-season storm, hundreds of thousands of birds depart their staging areas simultaneously, flying directly to their wintering grounds.

But if you're a duck hunter, a grand passage is not what you want to see. You'd much rather have the birds filter through gradually, stopping off to rest and feed along the way. Fortunately, the latter scenario is much more common than the former.

Not all species of ducks migrate at the same time. As a rule, puddlers migrate before divers, but there is considerable variation within each of these groups (see migration timetables, opposite). Blue-winged teal, for instance, migrate earlier than wigeon, and mallards migrate later yet.

Nor do all duck species follow the same migration route. Most hunters envision migration to be a north-south phenomenon but, in truth, there is nearly as much east-west movement.

Nobody knows for sure what spurs the migration, but early migrants seem to fly mainly by the calendar. They depart on approximately the same date each year, regardless of the weather. Late migrants, on the other hand, stay around until adverse weather, frozen water or a shortage of food forces them to move out. In a typical year, successive low-pressure systems over a period of several weeks will each move a fraction of the birds.

Waterfowl have a strong homing instinct. They return to the same wintering areas each fall and the same breeding areas each spring. They follow the same migration corridors, using the position of the sun and stars, the earth's magnetic field and visual landmarks to find their way.

These migration corridors should not be confused with *flyways,* which are administrative divisions, not actual flight paths. For waterfowl-management purposes, North America has been divided into four major flyways: the Pacific, Central, Mississippi and Atlantic. Some species of waterfowl cross two or three flyways when traveling from their breeding areas to their wintering grounds.

Migrating ducks normally fly at high altitudes; they have been spotted as high as 20,000 feet. Like airliners, they commonly ascend above dense fog banks to reach clear skies and favorable winds. But under low-visibility conditions, they fly much lower, sometimes only a little above the treetops.

Most duck species migrate at night. Flying at speeds of 40 to 60 mph, they can cover great distances in a short time. Some species travel only a few hundred miles to coastal wintering grounds; others fly thousands of miles to reach wintering areas in the southern hemisphere. Pintails banded in Alaska, for instance, have been shot in Guatemala, about 5000 miles away.

Pacific Flyway

Atlantic Flyway

Mississippi Flyway

Central Flyway

Migration Timetables

PUDDLE & DIVER DUCK FALL MIGRATION								
AUGUST		SEPTEMBER			OCTOBER			NOVEMBER
EARLY	LATE	EARLY	MID	LATE	EARLY	MID	LATE	EARLY
King Eider	Wigeon Pintail	Blue-winged Teal Cinnamon Teal Shoveler Oldsquaw	Common Eider Harlequin	Wood duck Gadwall Black duck Canvasback Black Scoter Whitewing Scoter Surf Scoter Lesser Scaup Greater Scaup Ruddy duck Ringneck	Barrow's Goldeneye Redhead	Green-winged Teal Bufflehead Hooded Merganser	Fulvous Whistling duck	Mallard Common Goldeneye Common Merganser Red-breasted Merganser

15

Puddle Ducks

As their name suggests, these ducks commonly frequent small, shallow bodies of water, but they may also be found on big water. Also called *dabblers*, they feed on or just below the surface, mainly on aquatic vegetation. They may skim food off the water, or they may tip up, submerging their upper body to feed while leaving their feet and rump pointing up. In fall, some puddle ducks also feed in grain fields. Their predominantly vegetable diet explains why they are considered better eating than most other ducks.

TIPPING UP, or dabbling, is the usual puddle duck feeding method.

How to Recognize Puddle Ducks

LEGS positioned near the center of the body give a puddler good balance, so it can easily walk and feed on land.

COLORED WING PATCHES are present on most puddlers. Most have a patch, called a *speculum*, on the wing's trailing edge. The speculum (arrow) is usually iridescent.

PUDDLE DUCKS commonly feed in harvested crop fields. The birds fly in to feed in the morning, fly back to the water to rest in midday, then return to the feeding fields in late afternoon. In cold weather, they may make several feeding flights during the day.

LARGE, POWERFUL WINGS (opposite) make it possible for puddlers to jump from the water almost vertically.

MALLARD. The distinctive drake, or greenhead, has an iridescent green head with an olive-green bill, a white neck ring and a rusty-colored breast. The belly and sides are silvery white; the back, gray. The hen, or susie (inset), is mottled brown overall, with a lighter belly and darker back. Her bill is orange with black blotches. Both sexes have orange legs and feet, and a blue-violet speculum with white margins. Juveniles resemble adult females, but the young males begin to show adult colors by early fall. Drakes measure 20 to 28 inches long and weigh 2 to 4 pounds; hens, 18 to 25 inches long and $1\frac{1}{2}$ to $3\frac{1}{2}$ pounds. The hen and drake both make quacking sounds, although the hen's call is much louder and higher in pitch.

MALLARD

Mallards are the most popular of all waterfowl. Most hunters set decoys in wetlands and use mallard calls to lure the birds into shooting range. Mallards are also hunted in crop fields, which can draw in thousands of birds.

Gregarious, highly vocal birds, mallards call frequently to entice other ducks into landing nearby.

In addition to corn, soybeans, wheat and other grains, mallards feed on rice and a wide variety of aquatic plants, including pondweeds, coontail, wild millet, sedges, canary grass, bulrushes and smartweed. When migrating and while on the wintering grounds, mallards often feed in grain fields in the morning, move to ponds and wetlands to loaf in midday, then return to feed on grain in late afternoon.

Mallards have the most extensive breeding range of any North American duck, nesting through most of the United States, and from eastern Canada to northern Alaska. The largest breeding populations are found in the prairie pothole region of the United States and Canada.

Breeding begins in the first year. Mallards are polygamous, and several drakes may attempt to breed with a single hen. Mallards prefer to nest in large sloughs and marshes, but they adapt easily to urban areas, often nesting in heavily used parks.

In an upland area, usually within 100 yards of water, the hen scrapes out a depression in dead vegetation, adding grass and twigs to complete the base of the nest. She lays 9 to 12 buff-colored eggs, cushioning them with down plucked from her breast. The eggs hatch in about 28 days.

In winter, mallards in the North are drawn to open-water rivers and lakes near agricultural fields. They move south only when freezing water forces them to leave. In the South, they are also found in wooded swamps. The largest wintering population is located in the south-central states and Mexico, although wintering birds can be found across most of the United States.

AMERICAN BLACK DUCK

Black ducks are normally hunted in and around coastal estuaries and bays, with the same techniques used for mallards. They look like dark-colored hen mallards, but they are considerably warier than mallards and often more difficult to draw in with decoys.

Equally at home in fresh- and saltwater marshes, black ducks eat a wide range of foods, including crustaceans and aquatic plants, such as wigeon grass and eelgrass. They also feed on acorns and, occasionally, small grains.

The primary breeding range includes the northern states, from Minnesota eastward, as well as the eastern half of Canada.

Like mallards, black ducks begin breeding in their first year. They prefer isolation and vigorously defend their breeding territory. Black ducks breed in brushy cover near fresh- or saltwater marshes.

The hen returns to the same nesting area each year, often choosing a location within a few yards of the previous year's nesting site. She scrapes a depression in the ground, then lines it with dead plant material. Black ducks also may nest on man-made platforms, on muskrat houses or in the crotches of trees. The hen lays about 9 creamy white eggs and cushions them with her own down. The eggs hatch in approximately 26 days.

Black ducks begin the fall migration in September and October, normally reaching their wintering areas in November and December. Most birds spend the winter on coastal bays and marshes, but some prefer open rivers and lakes. The largest wintering concentration is along the Atlantic coast, from Maine to South Carolina, but smaller concentrations can be found in several other southern states. Some winter as far north as the Maritime Provinces.

AMERICAN BLACK DUCK. The overall color of the black duck, also called the black mallard, is brownish black; the head and neck are a lighter brown, with a dark streak running through the eye. The speculum is blue with black edges, in contrast to the white-edged speculum on the mallard. The undersides of the wings are white. The hen and drake are nearly identical, but the drake's bill is bright yellow with a dark center; the hen's, olive-green (inset). Both sexes have reddish orange legs and feet. Juveniles resemble adults, but the young male's bill lacks the dark center. Adults measure 19 to 24 inches long and weigh 2 to 3½ pounds. Drakes are slightly larger than hens. The calls of both sexes are nearly identical to those of the mallard.

GADWALL

These subtly beautiful birds are often taken incidentally by mallard hunters. Although gadwalls are not particularly vocal, they readily respond to mallard decoys and calls.

The gadwall's favorite foods include the stems and leaves of aquatic plants, such as pondweeds, coontail, wigeon grass, muskgrass and eelgrass.

The prairie pothole region is the prime breeding area for gadwalls, but breeding populations can also be found in the Great Plains and Rocky Mountain states, Alaska and the eastern Great Lakes area.

Most birds breed during their first year. Because they migrate northward later than most other puddle-duck species, gadwalls are late nesters. The hen chooses a nesting site around a small prairie wetland. Typically, the nest is constructed in thick, tall vegetation near water, often on an island. She scrapes a shallow depression, lines it with dead vegetation and down, then lays about 10 creamy white eggs, which hatch in approximately 24 days.

The fall migration begins in September. Gadwalls generally fly at night, with most birds arriving on their wintering grounds in October and November. They winter on saltwater marshes and estuaries, and on freshwater marshes and rivers. Louisiana is home to the largest wintering population, but the birds also winter throughout much of the South and most of the Atlantic and Pacific coastal states.

GADWALL. The drake has gray-barred side feathers, accounting for the name gray duck. It also has a white belly and a black rump. The speculum is white, framed by black and brown feathers. The bill is black. The hen's back is brown; her sides, tan (inset). The undersides are light, and the bill is dull orange with a gray center streak. The white speculum of the hen is not as pronounced as that of the drake. Both sexes have yellowish orange legs and feet. Juveniles resemble adult hens, but in late fall the young males develop their adult plumage. Adults measure 18 to 22 inches long and weigh 1½ to 2½ pounds. Drakes are a little larger than hens. Drakes make short "nheck" calls and low whistles; hens, a mallardlike "gag-ag-ag-ag" call.

AMERICAN WIGEON. This duck's common name, baldpate, comes from the drake's prominent white forehead and crown. The drake has a deep green streak running from the eye to the back of the head. The back, sides and chest are pinkish brown; the undersides, white. Pronounced white shoulder patches are clearly visible in flight. The hen's sides and chest are chestnut-colored; her back, gray-brown (inset). Both sexes have blue-gray legs and feet. The bill is blue-gray with a black tip. Juvenile birds resemble adult hens. Adults measure 18 to 23 inches long and weigh 1 to 2½ pounds. Drakes are slightly larger than hens. Drakes make a three-note "wh-ee-oo" whistle; hens are normally silent.

AMERICAN WIGEON

The wigeon's breeding territory includes nearly all of Alaska, much of the western United States and western Canada. A small breeding population can be found in a band stretching across northern Canada into upper New England.

Wigeon begin breeding in their first year. They nest primarily around prairie marshes, ponds and shallow lakes. The hen typically nests in a clump of brushy cover near water. She builds her nest using grasses and down plucked from her own breast, then lays 8 or 9 creamy white eggs, which hatch in approximately 24 days.

Like gadwalls, wigeon are a secondary species for mallard hunters. They readily responds to mallard calls and decoy spreads.

Wigeon feed mainly on stems and leafy portions of aquatic plants. They also graze on upland grasses and legumes.

These ducks are early fall migrants, leaving the northern nesting grounds in mid-August and reaching stopover areas by September. By December, most birds have arrived on the wintering grounds. Wigeon winter on bays and estuaries, in all the coastal states, as well as in British Columbia and Mexico. The largest wintering concentrations are in the Central Valley of California and the extensive coastal marshes of Louisiana.

WOOD DUCK. The woodie is perhaps the most beautiful of all ducks. The drake has a ruddy red chest and a blue, white and iridescent green head with a pronounced crest. Its flanks are tawny; the undersides, whitish. The bill is reddish, with a yellow ring at the base, a black tip and a white patch on top. The hen has a less pronounced crest. Her bill is dull gray with a black tip, and her eye is circled by a white ring. Her back is dark brown, and the sides are mottled with tan and gray. The undersides are whitish. Both sexes have a blue speculum, and the legs and feet are yellow, though the color is duller in hens. Juveniles resemble adult hens, but, in fall, young males develop their adult plumage. Adults measure 15 to 21 inches long and weigh 1⅓ to 2 pounds. Drakes are slightly larger than hens. The hen makes a distinctive, high-pitched "woo-eek" squeal.

WOOD DUCK

Prized for its striking beauty, the highly maneuverable wood duck poses a difficult target when flying through the trees. Many wood ducks are taken incidentally to mallard hunting, but jump-shooting is a popular technique around small rivers and ponds. Some hunters attract the birds with wood-duck decoys and wood-duck whistles.

Wood ducks feed heavily on acorns from pin and white oaks. Lacking acorns, they will eat hickory nuts, corn and seeds from a variety of other plants, including bald cypress, button bush, bur reed and arrow arum.

The breeding range includes most of the eastern half of the United States, the West Coast states, and portions of central Canada and British Columbia. Pockets of breeding birds are also found in the Great Plains states.

Most wood ducks breed in their first year. They nest around marshes, rivers and ponds in densely wooded areas. The hen lays her eggs in an old woodpecker hole or other tree cavity, which she lines with her own down. Wood ducks also nest in man-made nesting boxes. The average clutch consists of about 12 beige eggs, although several hens may lay their eggs in the same nest. The hen incubates the eggs for about 30 days.

Wood ducks breeding in the South generally do not migrate, but birds in the northern part of the breeding range begin to migrate in September, reaching their winter destinations by mid-November. Most eastern wood ducks spend the winter in the southeastern United States and into Mexico. In the West, most wood ducks winter in the Sacramento Valley of California and along the west coast of Mexico. The birds usually winter in wooded wetlands.

NORTHERN PINTAIL The pintail, or sprig, is named for the drake's long tail. His head and neck are chocolate brown, with a white stripe running up both sides of the neck. The chest, belly and throat are white. The back and sides are grayish, growing darker near the tail. The speculum is green. The hen (inset) is a mottled brown, with a light belly. Her tail, though pointed, is not as long as the drake's. The speculum is brownish. Both sexes have dark gray legs and feet, and bluish gray bills. Juvenile birds resemble adult hens, but young males lack the long tail. Drakes measure 23 to 30 inches long and weigh 1½ to 3 pounds; hens, 21 to 25 inches long and 1⅓ to 2½ pounds. The hen's call is similar to that of the hen mallard; drakes make a subtle "preep-preep" whistle.

NORTHERN PINTAIL

These graceful, slender-winged birds are the favorite of many western duck hunters. They are hunted in much the same way as mallards. Some hunters use a mallard call to imitate the hen; others, a pintail whistle to mimic the drake.

Pintails feed heavily on rice and small grains, including wheat, oats and barley. They also eat invertebrates and many types of aquatic vegetation.

The pintail's extensive breeding range, surpassed in size only by that of the mallard, includes much of the western United States, Canada and Alaska. The largest breeding population is found in the prairie pothole region.

Most pintails breed in their first year. They usually nest along marshy shorelines of lakes and slow-moving streams, usually within 40 yards of water. Some nests, however, are a mile or more away. The nest, a shallow depression scraped in the ground and lined with vegetation and down, is usually made in an open area with low vegetation. The hen lays about 8 pale gray to olive-green eggs, which hatch in approximately 23 days.

Pintails begin the fall migration in August and, by October or November, most have reached their wintering grounds. They winter throughout the southern United States, the Caribbean islands, Mexico and parts of Central America. In winter, they prefer freshwater marshes and lakes, and coastal bays and estuaries.

BLUE-WINGED TEAL

These early migrants are commonly taken over mallard decoys set on shallow marshes or ponds, or by jump-shooting. Blue-winged teal respond well to mallard calls.

The bluewing's diet consists mainly of aquatic plants, such as muskgrass, wigeon grass, coontail, duckweeds and pondweeds. They also eat aquatic invertebrates.

The breeding range includes the northern half of the United States, many of the central states, parts of Alaska and much of southern Canada. The prairie pothole region contains the largest concentration of breeding birds.

Bluewings usually breed in their first year. They prefer to nest on prairie grasslands near ponds and marshes. The hen scrapes a bowl-like depression in the ground and lines it with grasses and down. She lays about 10 creamy tan eggs, which hatch in approximately 24 days. The drake stays with the hen until the third week of incubation.

Bluewing drakes head south from late August to early September, a few weeks before the hens. Most arrive on their wintering grounds in October and November.

In the United States, bluewings winter on coastal backwaters in California, the Gulf Coast states and Arkansas. Wintering birds are also found throughout Mexico and as far south as northern South America.

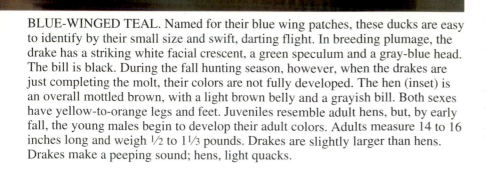

BLUE-WINGED TEAL. Named for their blue wing patches, these ducks are easy to identify by their small size and swift, darting flight. In breeding plumage, the drake has a striking white facial crescent, a green speculum and a gray-blue head. The bill is black. During the fall hunting season, however, when the drakes are just completing the molt, their colors are not fully developed. The hen (inset) is an overall mottled brown, with a light brown belly and a grayish bill. Both sexes have yellow-to-orange legs and feet. Juveniles resemble adult hens, but, by early fall, the young males begin to develop their adult colors. Adults measure 14 to 16 inches long and weigh ½ to 1⅓ pounds. Drakes are slightly larger than hens. Drakes make a peeping sound; hens, light quacks.

GREEN-WINGED TEAL. The greenwing is the smallest North American puddle duck. The drake has a rusty head with a brilliant green patch running from the eye down the neck, and a green speculum. The buff chest is flecked with brown and is framed by a white bar that separates the chest from the gray back and sides. The undersides are white; the legs and feet, brownish gray; the bill, dark gray. In fall, when the drakes are completing the molt,

their colors are not yet fully developed. The hen (inset) has mottled brown plumage overall, with white undersides. Juveniles resemble adult females, but, by late fall, the young males develop their adult colors. Adults measure 13 to 15 inches long and weigh ½ to 1 pound. The drake makes a loud "preep-preep" call; the hen, an occasional hurried quack.

GREEN-WINGED TEAL

Greenwings often challenge hunters by swooping low over decoys, only to rise and fly away without landing. These little ducks are deceptively fast and often fly in small, tight flocks. Most birds are taken incidentally by hunters seeking other puddle ducks.

Greenwings do most of their feeding on mud flats bordering wetlands. They eat seeds of moist-soil plants, such as smartweeds, nut-grasses and millets, but also feed on seeds from a variety of aquatic plants, including bulrushes, spike rushes and pondweeds.

The breeding range includes most of Alaska and Canada, and the prairie pothole region of the United States. The birds usually nest on prairie grasslands with marshes and ponds, on tundra or around the fringes of northern lakes in forested areas.

Greenwings normally breed in their first year. A secretive nester, the hen chooses a nesting site 50 to 100 feet from water, in a clump of dense grass or brushy cover. After constructing a grass nest and lining it with down, she lays 8 or 9 creamy white eggs, which hatch in about 21 days.

Unlike bluewings, greenwings often stay on their northern breeding grounds until late fall. They prefer to migrate at night, traveling in flocks of 100 or more birds. Most arrive on the wintering grounds in late November.

Greenwings winter on lakes and rivers throughout most of the South and Pacific Northwest, in some of the Rocky Mountain states and in Mexico. They also winter in coastal estuaries and bays.

CINNAMON TEAL

The twisting, darting flight of the cinnamon teal makes it a challenging target for western hunters. Most of the birds are taken incidentally by water-fowlers hunting mallards and pintails with decoys and calls.

The favorite foods of cinnamon teal include seeds of bulrushes and saltgrass and seeds and leaves of

pondweed. They also eat mollusks and other aquatic invertebrates.

The highest breeding concentration is near Utah's Great Salt Lake, but the breeding range also includes most of the western states, extending into Mexico and slightly into Canada. Cinnamon teal prefer to breed around marshes and freshwater lakes bordered with emergent vegetation.

Most birds begin to breed in their first year. After breeding, the hen seeks out a dense stand of grasses or rushes, where she constructs a nest lined with vegetation. She lays about 9 pinkish eggs, which she cushions with her own down. The eggs hatch in about 23 days.

Like bluewings, cinnamon teal are early migrants, departing the breeding areas in late August and early September. They arrive on the wintering grounds in late November and December. Most cinnamon teal winter on the marshes and lakes of Mexico, Central America and South America, but a few spend the winter in the southwestern United States. They sometimes winter on lakes at high altitude.

CINNAMON TEAL. This duck gets its name from the cinnamon color of the drake. In full breeding plumage, the drake has a powder blue shoulder patch and an irides-cent green speculum. The bill is black; the legs and feet, orange. During fall, when drakes are completing the molt, their colors are not yet fully developed. The hen (inset), often confused with the hen bluewing, is an over-all mottled brown, with a darker brown back and lighter buff undersides. She has a large, powder blue shoulder patch, a dark gray bill, and dull yellowish legs and feet. Juveniles resemble adult hens, but, by early fall, the young males begin to develop their reddish adult colors. Adults measure 14 to 17 inches long and weigh ½ to 1 pound. Drakes are slightly larger than hens. Both sexes quack softly and make a variety of clucking sounds.

NORTHERN SHOVELER. Named for its unique spoon-shaped bill, this duck is easily identified at close range. The drake is colorful, with an iridescent green head, white breast, chestnut flanks, green speculum and large powder blue shoulder patch. The bill is black. The hen resembles the hen mallard, but the bill is dull gray to brown. The

legs and feet of both sexes are orangish. Juveniles resemble adult hens, but, by early fall, young males develop the colorful adult plumage. Adults measure 17 to 20 inches long and weigh 1 to 2 pounds. Drakes are slightly larger than hens. Hen shovelers quack softly; drakes occasionally make a hollow-sounding "g'dunk-g'dunk g'dunk."

NORTHERN SHOVELER

other puddle duck. They strain water through their large, spoon-shaped bill to extract plankton and other small organisms and skim the surface of the mud for insects, mollusks and other invertebrates. They also eat duckweed, pondweeds and wigeon grass.

Shovelers begin breeding in their first year. With the help of the drake, the hen chooses a nesting site in a shortgrass prairie or hay field, often very close to her previous year's site and usually near water. She constructs a nest of matted vegetation, lining it with her own down. She lays 6 to 13 pale green eggs, which hatch in about 24 days.

A fully plumed drake shoveler is one of the most colorful of all ducks, but the bird's dark, often strong-tasting meat explains why hunters hold it in such low regard. Most shovelers are taken by hunters seeking other puddle ducks.

Shovelers breed around shallow lakes, marshes and seasonally flooded ponds with muddy margins. They winter on brackish or saltwater bays and lagoons. Their diet includes more small animal life than any

Shovelers breed from the prairies of western Minnesota to northwestern Alaska, but most are found in the prairie provinces of Alberta, Saskatchewan and Manitoba. They also breed in the Great Lakes region. These birds are early migrants, beginning the fall migration in early September and reaching the wintering areas by late November. They winter in California, the extreme southern United States and Mexico.

FULVOUS WHISTLING DUCK

Highly vocal in flight, the fulvous whistling duck is named for its whistling call.

Although this duck has one of the widest global distributions of any waterfowl species, it is seldom seen by hunters in the United States. Most are shot incidentally by hunters seeking other ducks.

Found on freshwater lakes and marshes, coastal saltwater marshes and flooded rice fields, fulvous whistling ducks prefer a rice diet but also eat acorns, grasses and grass seeds. Large flocks often fly into rice fields at sunset.

Fulvous whistling ducks mate for life, typically breeding in their first year. Using vegetation, the hen builds a nest a few inches above water, usually in a rice field or fringe of a marsh. She lays about 12 whitish eggs, which hatch in approximately 25 days. The drake helps raise the brood.

Besides North and South America, fulvous whistling ducks are found in India and eastern Africa. In North America, the birds breed in northern Mexico and in parts of Florida, Louisiana, Texas and California. Birds in the northern part of the range may migrate in late October and November to marshes in the southern part of the range. Southern birds seldom migrate.

FULVOUS WHISTLING DUCK. With its long neck and legs, the fulvous whistling duck, or fulvous tree duck, looks like no other puddle duck found in the continental United States. In both sexes, the neck and sides of the head are reddish brown; the crown, dark brown. Light streaks separate the dark brown back from the tawny sides and belly. The bill, legs and feet are blue-gray. Juveniles resemble adult birds, although their plumage is slightly duller. Adults measure 16 to 18 inches long and weigh 1 to 2 pounds. Drakes are slightly larger than hens. The fulvous whistling duck has a distinctive "k-weeoo" call.

MOTTLED DUCK

Seldom seen by the average waterfowler, mottled ducks are occasionally taken by hunters seeking mallards or other puddle ducks. They readily respond to mallard decoy spreads and calls.

Mottled ducks feed primarily on fish, snails, crayfish and aquatic insects, which explains the duck's somewhat strong flavor. Other important items in the diet include rice, wild millet and pondweeds.

The breeding range of the mottled duck includes most of Florida and a stretch of the Gulf Coast from Alabama into northern Mexico. The birds usually nest in the vicinity of freshwater marshes and flooded grasslands, and sometimes around brackish coastal marshes and estuaries.

The birds begin to breed in their first year. The hen often chooses a nesting site very close to where she was hatched. She typically builds a nest on a clump of cordgrass close to water, then lays 9 to 11 eggs, which hatch in about 26 days.

Although they do not migrate in the same fashion as most other ducks, mottled ducks move inland during September and October to feed in rice fields. They return to coastal marshes in winter.

MOTTLED DUCK. This puddle duck, also called the Florida mallard, is easily confused with the black duck and hen mallard. But it is slightly lighter in color than the black duck and can be distinguished from the hen mallard by the black rather than white borders on the bluish speculum. Drakes have olive-green bills; hens, orange bills with dark spots. Both sexes have orange legs and feet. Juveniles resemble adults. Adults measure 17½ to 24 inches long and weigh 2 to 3 pounds. Drakes are slightly larger than hens. Mottled ducks make quacking sounds similar to those of the mallard.

Diving Ducks

With legs positioned farther back on the body, these ducks are more adept at diving beneath the surface than are puddle ducks. Their feet are larger for their size, so they are better underwater swimmers. The leg position also makes it more difficult for them to walk on land, explaining why they seldom feed in agricultural fields. The diet of most divers consists mainly of invertebrates and fish, explaining their strong taste. But some, such as canvasbacks and redheads, feed heavily on wild celery and other aquatic vegetation, and are considered better eating.

Sea ducks, a subcategory of diving duck, differ from ordinary divers in that they spend most of their life in coastal areas. They have remarkable diving ability, with some species descending to depths of more than 200 feet to feed on mollusks, crustaceans and fish.

Mergansers, often called *fish ducks*, are also classified as a subcategory of diving duck. They feed even more heavily on fish than other divers, and their serrated bill is ideal for catching and holding small fish until they can be swallowed whole. Their crested head easily distinguishes them from other diving ducks.

Diving ducks plunge well beneath the surface to feed

How to Recognize Diving Ducks

RUNNING on the water helps divers gain enough speed for take-off. Their small wings provide less lift than those of puddlers.

LARGE FEET and legs positioned far back on the body account for the diving ability of these ducks.

WHITE to dark gray wing patches are found on most diving duck species.

FLYING LOW over the water in tight flocks is typical behavior among most diver species. In flight, divers can be distinguished from puddlers by their shorter, faster wingbeat.

31

CANVASBACK. Cans resemble redheads, but have a longer, straighter profile from the crown to the tip of the bill. The sides and back are whitish gray, and are much lighter than those of the drake redhead. The belly is white; the tail, rump and bib, black. The hen's body is an overall drab gray, with a sandy brown head (inset). Both sexes have a black bill and bluish gray feet. Juvenile females closely resemble adult hens. Young males have brownish heads and chests until they develop their adult plumage in fall. Adults measure 18 to 22 inches long and weigh 2 to 3½ pounds. Drakes are slightly larger than hens. The drake makes a low croak; the hen, a sharp "krrr" or quack.

CANVASBACK

Canvasback are among the most highly prized of all waterfowl. Not only are they the fastest flyers, they're arguably the best eating. Hunting for cans is best in late season, especially in the foulest of weather. Although not particularly vocal, cans respond well to diver calls and diver decoy setups.

Cans have a strong preference for wild celery; in fact, their species name, *valisineria*, is derived from the plant's Latin name. But celery has been decimated throughout much of their range, so cans now feed largely on sago pondweed, arrowhead root, bulrush seeds, mollusks, crustaceans and fish.

Canvasbacks breed from central Alaska through western Canada to Minnesota, and in some of the western states. Most, however, are found in the prairie pothole region. Cans prefer prairie marshes for nesting.

If there is plenty of water and cover on the breeding grounds, cans breed in their first year. Otherwise, they wait until their second year. They usually nest in dense emergent vegetation, primarily cattails and bulrushes, along the fringes of marshes. The hen uses the vegetation to build a large, bulky nest, then lays a clutch of about 8 greenish eggs, which hatch in 23 to 25 days. Redhead hens sometimes lay their eggs in canvasback nests, causing the canvasback hen to lay fewer eggs.

Canvasbacks begin the fall migration in late September, stopping along the way on large lakes and rivers, sometimes for several weeks at a time. By January, most birds have reached their wintering grounds.

Cans generally winter on large lakes and in coastal bays and estuaries in the Atlantic and Pacific coast states, the Gulf Coast states and Mexico. Smaller wintering concentrations are found around the Great Lakes and in Oklahoma, Arkansas and Arizona.

During the drought of the 1980s, canvasback numbers dropped so low that the hunting season was closed for several years. Rising water levels and wild celery restoration efforts have improved the population enough to warrant reopening the season.

REDHEAD. Like the drake can, the drake redhead has a reddish head, black bib and rump, and a white belly, but it is slightly smaller with a more rounded forehead profile, and a darker back and sides. The bill is blue-gray, with a black tip. The hen (inset) has a reddish brown head, neck and breast, drab brown back and sides, and white undersides. The pattern on her bill is slightly less conspicuous than on the male. Both sexes have gray legs and feet. Juveniles resemble hens until fall, when the young males begin to develop the brilliant adult plumage. Adults measure 18 to 22 inches long and weigh 1½ to 3 pounds. Drakes are slightly larger than hens. The drake makes distinctive "whee-ough" and rolling "rrrrr" sounds; the hen, a sharp quacking sound.

REDHEAD

Diving-duck enthusiasts rank the redhead nearly as high as the canvasback. Redheads bear a superficial resemblance to cans and their mild-tasting meat is equally good.

Like many other diving ducks, redheads respond to diver decoy lines and diver calls.

These birds consume more plant material than most diving ducks. They tend to feed in relatively shallow water, where they seek out pondweeds, coontail, wild celery, muskgrass, bulrushes and duckweed.

Redheads nest primarily in lakes and marshes in the prairie pothole region, but significant numbers also breed in the area around the Great Salt Lake. Smaller breeding populations are found in other western states, around the Great Lakes, in Alaska and in Minnesota.

Birds hatched early in the season often breed in their first year, but those hatched late generally do not breed until their second year. They prefer nesting sites in emergent vegetation in shallow water, but may lay their eggs in the nests of other ducks. The hen uses vegetation to weave a bowl-shaped nest, which is lined with down and anchored to cattails or bulrushes. She lays 10 to 12 buff-colored eggs, which hatch in 24 to 28 days.

Redheads depart their breeding grounds in September and October and reach their wintering areas by November and December. The birds have a large wintering range that includes lakes and reservoirs across most of the South, in the Ozarks, in nearly all of the western states and throughout most of Mexico. They also winter on tidal bays and estuaries along the Atlantic Seaboard.

LESSER SCAUP

Lesser scaup are still the most numerous species of diving duck, but, in recent years, their population has undergone a marked decline in spite of improving water levels in most of their breeding range.

Easily lured in by a standard line of diver decoys and a diver call, lesser scaup are considered one of the least wary diving ducks.

Important foods include aquatic invertebrates, such as clams and snails, but the birds also eat large quantities of smartweed and aquatic plants, mainly wild celery, wigeon grass and bulrushes. Their fondness for vegetation explains why they are not as strong-tasting as many other diving ducks.

Lesser scaup breed in the prairie pothole region, parts of the Northwest, western Canada and most of Alaska. They usually nest near prairie marshes, and around shallow ponds and lakes fringed with emergent vegetation.

The birds seldom breed before their second year. Unlike most diving ducks, the hen builds her nest in an upland area, using grasses, sedges and other vegetation. She lays about 9 dark olive eggs, which hatch in approximately 25 days.

The fall migration begins in late September, and most birds arrive on their wintering areas between October and December. The birds winter on coastal bays and estuaries, and on large freshwater lakes throughout most of the coastal states and in Mexico. Lesser scaup often winter with greater scaup.

LESSER SCAUP. All scaup get their common name, bluebill, from the blue-gray bill, which has a black tip. The lesser scaup closely resembles its slightly larger cousin, the greater scaup, but the drake's head has a purplish rather than greenish sheen. The drake's neck, chest and rump are black; the sides and undersides, white. The back is mottled with black and white. The hen (inset) is dark brown overall; the head and breast are slightly darker than the sides and back. The undersides are whitish. A white ring circles the base of the bill. Both sexes have blue-gray legs and feet, and a long, white speculum. Juveniles resemble adult hens. Adults measure 15 to 18 inches long and weigh 1 to 2½ pounds. Drakes are slightly larger than hens. Drakes make soft whistling notes; hens, low growling sounds.

GREATER SCAUP. This bird is nearly identical to the lesser scaup, but is a little larger. Like the drake lesser, the drake greater has a black chest and rump, white sides and undersides, and a back mottled with black and white. But his head has a greenish sheen rather than a purple hue. The hen's overall color is dark brown with whitish undersides (inset) and a white ring around the base of the bill.

Both sexes have blue-gray legs and feet, a blue-gray bill with a black tip and a white speculum. Juveniles resemble adult hens. Adults measure 15½ to 20 inches long and weigh 1½ to 3 pounds. Drakes are slightly larger than hens. Both sexes make soft croaking sounds; the drake also coos and whistles.

GREATER SCAUP

Far less abundant than its slightly smaller cousin, the lesser scaup, the greater scaup has similar habits and is generally hunted using the same techniques.

Clams are the food of choice for these diving ducks, but they also feed on a variety of aquatic plants, including pondweeds, wild celery and sea lettuce.

Greater scaup rarely breed before their second year. They have a smaller, more northerly breeding range than lessers, including most of Alaska and the Yukon, and parts of northern Canada. They generally nest around tundra lakes and ponds, with the hen choosing a nesting site on an elevated mound with a good view of the surrounding area. She uses grasses to build a bowl-shaped nest and may lay her eggs in the nest of another duck. The average clutch consists of 9 olive-colored eggs, which hatch in 23 to 28 days.

The birds begin the fall migration in September, reaching the wintering grounds in October. They winter on coastal bays and estuaries along most of the Atlantic, Pacific and Gulf coasts, and on the lower Great Lakes.

RING-NECKED DUCK

The ringneck's name is misleading, because the chestnut ring around the drake's neck is visible only at close range.

Ringnecks have a mild taste and are popular among hunters. They eagerly respond to lines of diver decoys and diver calls.

Favorite foods include the leaves and seeds of pondweeds, duckweed, coontail and a variety of other aquatic plants. Although they are diving ducks, ringnecks prefer water just a few feet deep, feeding in seasonal pools, shallow ponds and marshes.

Ringnecks breed across much of Canada, but are most concentrated in Alberta, Saskatchewan and Manitoba. Breeding populations are also found in Alaska, the Pacific Northwest, the Rocky Mountain states, the Great Lakes region and upper New England.

Unlike many diving ducks, ringnecks generally breed in their first year. Typically, the hen chooses a nesting site on a pond in a wooded area, often near an island, where she builds her nest on a small cluster of floating vegetation. She lays 8 or 9 olive eggs, which hatch in 25 to 29 days. The drake sometimes stays with the hen through incubation.

The fall migration begins in September, with most of the birds reaching wintering areas between October and December. The majority of ringnecks winter on large freshwater lakes in the southern United States and Mexico, but some are found on estuaries in most coastal states.

RING-NECKED DUCK. The drake has a black head with a purple-blue sheen and a vague chestnut-colored ring around the neck. The back and bib are black; the sides, grayish white; the belly, white. The slate gray bill is edged with white and has a white ring near the tip, accounting for the common name – ringbill. The hen has tan sides, a brown back and white belly. Her bill ring is less pronounced than on the drake. Juveniles resemble adult hens, though the young males have a more distinctive bill ring. Adults measure 16 to 18 inches long and weigh 1 to 2 pounds. Drakes are slightly larger than hens. The drake makes a low whistling note; the hen, a gentle rolling "rrrr."

BUFFLEHEAD

The chubby shape of this small diving duck accounts for its common name – butterball. These birds are not particularly popular among hunters because of their strong taste; most are taken incidentally by hunters pursuing other diving ducks.

The bufflehead's diet consists mostly of fish and aquatic

invertebrates, but they also feed on a variety of aquatic plants.

Buffleheads breed across the Alaskan interior, throughout most of Canada and in the northern Rockies and Cascades of the continental United States.

Most buffleheads begin breeding in their second year. They prefer to nest in holes in trees near water, often holes made by flickers in aspen trees. The hen lays about 9 creamy buff eggs, which hatch in approximately 30 days.

The fall migration begins in mid-October, with the birds arriving on wintering areas in November and December. Buffleheads winter on large lakes and rivers over most of the continental United States, except for the north-central states, and in northern Mexico. Wintering birds can also be found on coastal bays and estuaries.

BUFFLEHEAD. The drake's head is black with a green and purple sheen, and has a white, wedge-shaped patch behind the eye. The back is black; the sides and belly, white. The bill is blue-gray; the feet and legs, pinkish. The hen's head is dark brown with a small white patch behind the eye (inset). The back is dark brown; the sides, grayish; the belly, white. The legs and feet are grayish; the bill, a darker gray. Juveniles resemble adult hens, though they lack the white patch. Adults measure 13 to 16 inches long and weigh ¾ to 1½ pounds. Drakes are slightly larger than hens. The drake makes squeaky whistles and guttural notes; the hen, soft quacks.

COMMON GOLDENEYE. The bird is named for its yellowish gold eye. The drake has a black head with a greenish sheen, a round white spot in front of the eye and a black bill. A row of black and white streaked feathers separates the white chest and undersides from the black rump and back. The hen's head is dark brown, with no facial spot (inset). The sides and back are gray; the belly, white; the bill, dark with a yellowish tip. Both sexes have yellowish legs and feet. Juveniles resemble adult females. Adults measure 16 to 20 inches long and weigh 1½ to 3⅓ pounds. Drakes are slightly larger than hens. The drake makes a "jeee-ep" call; the hen, low guttural quacks.

COMMON GOLDENEYE

This duck's common name, whistler, comes from the whistling sound made by its wings. A big-water bird, it is usually hunted over long points by leading it in with strings of decoys. Its meat is strong-tasting, a result of the aquatic invertebrate and fish diet. It also eats aquatic

plants, including wild celery, pondweeds, water lily and bulrush seeds.

Common goldeneyes breed across most of Canada, in much of Alaska, and in parts of the extreme northern continental United States. They rarely mate before their second year. A hen typically nests in a tree cavity or man-made nest box in a wooded area around a slow-moving river or lake. She lays about 9 greenish blue eggs, which hatch in approximately 30 days. She may lay her eggs in the nest of another duck.

This hardy bird, one of the last migrants, remains in the breeding range until forced south by freezing waters. By late November, most birds have reached their wintering areas, which include large freshwater lakes throughout the United States and bays and estuaries along the Pacific coast of Alaska and Canada.

BARROW'S GOLDENEYE

The Barrow's goldeneye has a much smaller range than the common. It also makes loud whistling noises in flight, and its diet and taste are similar.

The birds breed around lakes and rivers in wooded, mountainous areas from Oregon and Wyoming to central Alaska, with some breeding on the tundra of northern Labrador and Quebec. The breeding habits are much like those of the common goldeneye.

Most birds leave the breeding grounds by early October, arriving on the wintering grounds from late October to early November. Drakes usually migrate before the hens. The birds winter on bays and estuaries along the Pacific coast from Alaska to central California and most of the Atlantic coast of Canada. Birds in mountainous regions do not migrate, spending the winter on any open water they can find.

BARROW'S GOLDENEYE. These birds resemble common goldeneyes, but the drake's eye spot is crescent-shaped rather than round, and his head has a purplish rather than greenish sheen. The black back, which has rows of white spots, extends farther down the sides. The hen's head is darker than the common goldeneye's, and her bill is orange-yellow, with a black base and tip (inset). Adults measure 16 to 20 inches long and weigh 1 to 2½ pounds. Drakes are slightly larger than hens. The bird's vocalizations are limited, but the drake sometimes makes a soft "ka-KAA" sound.

RUDDY DUCK

This small, chunky diver is easily identified by its upright, unusually stiff tail feathers. It swims very low in the water and, when threatened, escapes by sinking slowly out of sight. Ruddy ducks are mild-tasting, but are seldom intentionally sought by hunters.

The ruddy duck's diet consists mostly of plants, including pondweeds, wigeon grass and bulrush seeds, as well as larval aquatic insects. They prefer shallow water, usually feeding at depths of 2 to 10 feet.

Ruddy ducks breed in the western states and western Canada as well as the Great Lakes region. Most mate in their second year. The hen usually builds a floating nest on dense vegetation over shallow water on marshes and weedy lakes, but she may lay her eggs in the nest of another duck. The average clutch consists of 8 cream-colored eggs, which hatch in about 25 days.

The fall migration begins in September and, by December, most birds have reached their wintering areas, primarily freshwater marshes in the South. They also winter on bays along the Atlantic and Pacific coasts.

RUDDY DUCK. The drake's plumage varies seasonally. In summer, he has a chestnut body and neck, a black crown, large white cheek patches and a very broad, pale blue bill. In fall and winter, his color fades to resemble that of the hen, and his bill turns black. He retains the large white cheek patches. The hen (inset) is dusky brown overall, with a darker back, chest and crown, and buff-colored undersides. The whitish cheeks are streaked with brown, and the bill is dull blackish blue. Both sexes have gray legs and feet. Juveniles resemble adult hens. Adults measure 14½ to 16 inches long and weigh ½ to 1½ pounds. Drakes are slightly larger than hens. Ruddy ducks are generally silent.

HOODED MERGANSER

The drake hooded merganser, with its pronounced crest and distinctive black and white barring, ranks among the most handsome of all waterfowl. Like the other mergansers, it is seldom an intentional target of duck hunters.

The hooded merganser's diet consists mostly of crustaceans, frogs, aquatic insects

and fish. These birds usually feed near shore, and eat less fish than the other merganser species.

In the West, the breeding range extends from the Alaskan panhandle south into the mountains of Washington, Oregon, Idaho and Montana. The eastern breeding range includes southern Canada and much of the eastern United States, with the largest concentration found in the Great Lakes region.

Most birds begin to breed as two-year-olds. Nesting takes place around slow-moving rivers, small ponds and lakes in wooded areas. The hen typically nests in a down-lined tree cavity, but will also nest in man-made nest boxes. Hens have been known to lay their eggs in another duck's nest. The average clutch consists of 10 white eggs, which hatch in about 32 days.

The fall migration begins in mid-October, with most birds reaching their wintering areas by November and December. The birds winter on rivers and lakes in the southeastern United States, on coastal marshes, bays and estuaries along the Atlantic Seaboard as far north as Cape Cod, and along the Pacific Seaboard from the Alaskan panhandle to the Baja Peninsula.

HOODED MERGANSER. The drake has a pronounced fan-shaped, black-and-white crest. The back is black with white stripes. The sides are brownish; the breast and belly, white. The legs and feet are brownish yellow; the bill, black. The hen (inset) has a reddish brown crested head and a dark back. The belly is white; the sides, gray. The bill is blackish on top and yellowish below. The legs and feet are yellowish gray. Both sexes have white leading edges on the wings. Juvenile males do not develop adult plumage until the second winter. Juvenile females resemble adult hens, but the crest is less pronounced. Adults measure 16 to 19 inches long and weigh 1¼ to 2 pounds. Drakes are slightly larger than hens. Both sexes are normally silent, but they sometimes make coarse grunts and croaks.

COMMON MERGANSER

Often called the American merganser, this bird ranks behind only the common eider as the largest North American duck. Most are taken incidentally by hunters seeking other diving ducks. They feed primarily on small fish.

These birds breed in many western states, in the Great Lakes region and in a wide band across Canada and into Alaska. They generally do not breed until their second year. The hen prefers to nest in a tree cavity, usually near a pond or river in a wooded area, but she may nest in a rock crevice or small depression close to water. Most clutches consist of 10 or 11 cream-colored eggs, which hatch in about 30 days. Two hens sometimes share a single nest and raise the combined brood together.

Common mergansers readily cope with cold temperatures, so they are one of the last ducks to fly south in fall. They winter on large lakes and rivers throughout much of the United States into northern Mexico and on bays along the Pacific coast of Canada and Alaska. Most arrive in November or December.

COMMON MERGANSER. This large bird has the pointed bill characteristic of all mergansers. The drake has a dark green head with no crest, a black back, white sides and a white belly. The hen's crested head is brown; the back, chest and sides are gray; the belly, white (inset). Both sexes have red bills and feet. Juveniles resemble adult hens. Drakes measure 23 to 27 inches long and weigh 2 to 4½ pounds; hens, 21 to 26 inches long and 2 to 3 pounds. Both sexes sometimes make hoarse croaks.

RED-BREASTED MERGANSER

These birds resemble common mergansers, but are smaller and have a shaggy crest on the back of the head. Most are taken by waterfowlers seeking other ducks. The diet includes a wide variety of small fish, as well as crustaceans.

Redbreasts breed from Newfoundland to Alaska and south into Maine and the Great Lakes region. They begin to breed as two-year-olds, nesting in rocky, grassy or brushy cover around tundra ponds or lakes in wooded areas. The hen lays about 8 buff-colored eggs, which hatch in approximately 30 days.

Most birds migrate in November and reach their wintering areas by late December. They winter on bays and estuaries along most of the coastline of the United States, in some coastal areas of Canada and Mexico and on the Great Lakes.

RED-BREASTED MERGANSER. The drake has a crested green head, a reddish brown chest, a black back and a white belly. The hen (inset) has a reddish brown head with a less pronounced crest. The back and sides are gray; the belly, white. Both sexes have red feet and narrow red bills. Juveniles resemble adult hens. Adults measure 18 to 23 inches long and weigh 1½ to 3 pounds. Drakes are slightly larger than hens. Both sexes are relatively silent, although they occasionally make hoarse croaking sounds.

COMMON EIDER. The long, sloping bill gives this bird's head a distinctive wedge shape. The drake has a white neck, breast and back, with black flanks and undersides. The head is white with an olive nape and a white-streaked black crown. The bill is yellowish to olive, with a gray tip. The hen (inset) is tan, mottled with black, and has a grayish bill. Both sexes have grayish legs and feet. Juveniles resemble adult hens. Drakes measure 22½ to 26½ inches long and weigh 4 to 6½ pounds; hens, 21 to 25 inches long and 3 to 6 pounds. The hen makes quacking noises; the drake, an "ahOOoo" call.

COMMON EIDER

Common eiders eat mostly mollusks, crustaceans and fish. They generally feed in waters 4 to 10 feet deep, but may dive as deep as 60 feet.

Most common eiders breed near the coastlines of Alaska, the Canadian Arctic and Hudson Bay, and in scattered areas of eastern Canada.

The majority of the birds begin breeding in their third year. Hens form loose nesting colonies on the tundra or along rocky shorelines. A hen typically chooses a sheltered nesting site, using grasses and her own down to build a nest. The drake stands guard while the hen lays 3 or 4 buff-olive eggs, but leaves when she begins incubation, which lasts 26 to 28 days.

Sometimes called the American eider, the common eider is the largest North American duck. These colorful birds are prized by waterfowlers seeking an unusual trophy for taxidermy purposes. But they are difficult to hunt because they often are found far from shore. The standard hunting technique is to anchor a seaworthy boat well offshore and surround it with decoys.

The fall migration begins in mid-September, with birds arriving on the wintering grounds from mid-October to December. They winter on the coastal waters of Alaska and eastern Canada, usually on the open sea, out of sight of land.

KING EIDER. The drake is known for its unique, colorful head. A shield of orange and black feathers surrounds the top of the bill. The crown and back of the head are blue-gray; the cheeks, light green. The neck and breast are creamy white, and the rest of the body is black, except for small patches of white on the flanks and on the tops of the wings. Two stiff feathers project from the back. The legs and feet are yellowish orange. The hen (inset) is brown, marked with black crescents, and the olive-gray bill has no shield. The legs and feet are grayish. Juveniles resemble adult hens, but, by fall, young males begin to show the distinctive forehead. Adults measure 18 to 25 inches long and weigh 2¾ to 4¼ pounds. Drakes are slightly larger than hens. Both sexes make low croaking noises.

KING EIDER

The king eider's dramatic plumage makes it a favorite among bird collectors and a popular trophy duck among many waterfowlers. They are normally hunted using the techniques recommended for common eiders (opposite).

King eiders eat mostly invertebrates, and are extraordi-

nary divers – they have been known to feed at depths as great as 180 feet.

The king eider's breeding range includes coastal areas north of the Arctic Circle and the shores of Hudson Bay.

Most birds begin to breed in their second or third year. Unlike common eiders, kings prefer isolation when nesting. The hen chooses a dry tundra slope, usually overlooking a pool or lake, and sometimes on an island. She creates a down-lined depression, then lays 4 or 5 olive-colored eggs, which hatch in 23 or 24 days.

The fall migration begins in July or August, with drakes leaving the breeding range slightly before hens. The birds arrive on the wintering grounds from mid-September to December. They winter on rocky shorelines along the Pacific coast of Alaska and along the Atlantic coast, from Virginia to Labrador. Like common eiders, they spend most of the winter at sea.

HARLEQUIN DUCK

Harlequins are rarely hunted in the East, but, in the West, they are occasionally sought by specimen collectors, using traditional sea-duck hunting methods.

Crustaceans, mollusks, insects and fish comprise the bulk of the harlequin's diet. These birds dive and feed in turbulent waters, feeding along the bottom of swift streams and in heavy surf.

The harlequin duck rivals the wood duck as North America's most beautiful waterfowl. There are distinct Atlantic and Pacific populations, with the Pacific population being much larger. The Atlantic population has dropped so dramatically that the birds are considered endangered. The cause of this decline is unknown.

Atlantic birds breed in Iceland, Greenland and northeastern Canada; Pacific birds, from the central Rockies to northern Alaska. Unique among diving ducks, harlequins prefer to nest around cold, fast-moving streams, often in mountainous regions.

These birds first breed as two-year-olds. The hen constructs a simple nest of grass, twigs and down, usually under a shrub or among rocks along a stream. She lays about 5 cream-colored eggs, which hatch in 28 to 30 days. While the hen nests, the drake defends against intruders.

The fall migration, which begins in mid-September, involves a short movement to rocky seacoasts.

HARLEQUIN DUCK. The drake has blue-gray plumage over-all, with white streaks and patches, many bordered with black. The flanks are russet-colored, and the crown has a russet patch. The bill is bluish gray. The hen is dark brown overall, with a white belly and white patches on the head. Both sexes have grayish legs, feet and bills. Juveniles resemble the adult hen. Drakes measure 16 to 21 inches long and weigh 1⅓ to 1⅔ pounds; hens, 14 to 17 inches and 1 to 1⅓ pounds. The drake occasionally makes high-pitched squeaks; the hen, "ek-ek-ek" calls.

OLDSQUAW. This duck has four distinct plumages. In fall (shown), the drake's back is dark brown, with gray shoulders; the flanks and neck are white. The white head has tan cheek patches and a dark spot at the rear. The black bill has a pink band. Although the color is darker in the other phases, the bird always has a long, dark brown tail. The hen's color shift is less dramatic. The body and wings are mottled light and dark brown; the belly is white (inset).

In winter, the head is a patchy white and brown; in summer, it is dark. The tail is much shorter than the drake's, and the bill is gray. Both sexes have gray legs and feet. Juveniles look like hens, but, by fall, young males begin to resemble adults. Drakes are 19 to 23 inches long and weigh 2 to 2½ pounds; hens, 15 to 17 inches and 1½ to 2 pounds. One of the most vocal of all ducks, oldsquaws make a variety of yodeling, clucking and growling sounds.

OLDSQUAW

Crustaceans, mollusks, fish and insect larvae comprise most of the bird's diet. Oldsquaws regularly feed at depths of 20 to 30 feet and have been known to dive as deep as 200.

Oldsquaws breed across northern Alaska and the Canadian Arctic, and around Hudson Bay. They begin breeding in their second year. The hen typically chooses a nesting site on the tundra but close to the water's edge, usually along the seacoast or near a freshwater lake or pond. In a sheltered spot, she constructs a bowl-shaped nest using grasses and down, then lays about 7 cream-colored eggs, which hatch in approximately 26 days.

Although they are not often seen in North America, oldsquaws rank among the world's most numerous ducks. The distinctively colored drake oldsquaw is highly prized by waterfowl collectors. The birds are hunted using traditional sea-duck techniques.

Usually flying at night, oldsquaws begin the fall migration in early September, completing the journey by November or December. They winter on coastal bays along the Pacific and Atlantic Seaboards, and along the Gulf Coast from Louisiana to the Florida panhandle. Some oldsquaws also winter on the Great Lakes.

WHITE-WINGED SCOTER. This sea duck is named for its white wing patches. The drake has all-black plumage, except for the wing patch and a small white crescent around the eye. The orange-yellow bill has a dark knob at the base, and a reddish tip. The legs and feet are reddish orange. The hen's overall color is slightly lighter than the drake's, and her wing patch is smaller (inset). She has tannish patches on the cheeks, and a grayish bill with no knob. The legs and feet are grayish yellow to dull orange. Juveniles resemble adult hens, though the immature male has mottled white undersides. Drakes measure 21 to 23 inches long and weigh 3 to 4 pounds; hens, 19 to 22 inches and 2 to 3 pounds. The drake sometimes makes whistling calls; the hen, a raspy "karrr."

WHITE-WINGED SCOTER

The diet of the white-winged scoter includes mussels, crabs, crayfish and barnacles. The birds may dive to depths up to 90 feet while feeding.

Whitewings breed across much of the Alaskan interior and western Canada. They nest primarily around lakes and ponds surrounded by sparse woods.

Most birds first breed in their second or third year. The hen usually selects a nesting site near water, but occasionally can be found nesting hundreds of yards away. She typically builds a nest in a ground hollow, lining it with down and dead vegetation. Whitewings have also been known to use man-made nest boxes. The hen lays about 9 buff-colored eggs, which hatch in approximately 28 days.

The fall migration begins from late September to mid-October, with most birds arriving on wintering areas in December and January. Whitewings complete the migration later than any other scoter species.

In the West, whitewings winter along the Pacific coast from southern Alaska into the Baja Peninsula. In the East, they winter on the Great Lakes, along most of the Atlantic coast, and along the Gulf Coast, from Texas to the Florida panhandle.

Whitewings are the most numerous of the scoter species, and have the largest breeding range. You can hunt whitewings in traditional sea-duck fashion, by stringing long lines of decoys into open water to draw the birds into shooting range. Decoys may consist of nothing more than black jugs.

SURF SCOTER

This bird gets its name from its habit of feeding in turbulent water along the surf line. Surf scoters are hunted in the same fashion as whitewings.

The surf scoter feeds mainly on mollusks, crustaceans and aquatic insects. It also eats aquatic plants, including wigeon grass, pondweeds and eelgrass.

Surf scoters breed in Alaska and across northern Canada. They begin breeding in their second year. The hen builds a down-lined nest in marsh vegetation near a river, pond or lake in a sparsely wooded area, or under a bush far from the water. She lays 5 to 7 pinkish white eggs, which hatch in about 30 days.

The fall migration begins in late September to early October, and, by December, most birds have arrived on their wintering grounds. Surf scoters winter on the open ocean or in large bays along the Pacific coast from Alaska into the Baja Peninsula, along most of the Atlantic coast and along a small stretch of the Gulf Coast, from the Florida panhandle to Mississippi. They also winter on the Great Lakes.

SURF SCOTER. The drake is black except for white patches on the forehead and back of the neck. His colorful bill is red, white, yellow and black, with a noticeable hump in the middle. The hen (inset) is grayish brown overall, with a white belly, a small white patch below the eye and a large, grayish black bill. Both sexes have orange legs and feet. Juveniles resemble adult hens. Adults measure 17 to 21 inches long and weigh 1½ to 2½ pounds. Drakes are slightly larger than hens. Surf scoters are normally silent, but may make low croaks.

BLACK SCOTER

Named for the pure black plumage of the drake, the black scoter is also called the common scoter or American scoter. These birds are scarce, but a few are taken by hunters using the methods described for whitewings.

The breeding range includes portions of western and central Alaska, and isolated pockets in Newfoundland, Quebec and the Northwest Territories. The breeding habits and diet are similar to those of the surf scoter.

The fall migration begins in late September, with most birds arriving on the wintering grounds in December. Black scoters winter on bays along the Pacific coast from southern Alaska to California, along most of the Atlantic coast, along the Gulf Coast from Texas to the Florida panhandle and on the Great Lakes.

BLACK SCOTER. The drake is completely black, except for the prominent bright yellow knob on its bill. The hen (inset) is a mottled brown, with a darker cap and lighter cheeks and throat. Her black bill has no knob. Both sexes have dark gray legs and feet. Juveniles resemble adult hens, but the young male's belly is slightly lighter and is a mottled white. Adults measure 17 to 21 inches long and weigh 2 to 3 pounds. Drakes are slightly larger than hens. Both sexes make a musical "cour-loo" whistle.

Duck-Hunting Equipment & Skills

Shotguns

In years past, no "real" duck hunter would think of going afield with anything but a full-choke shotgun. Of course, a full-choke required a good shooting eye, but it would bring down the high fliers. With the ban on use of lead shot, however, preferences in duck-hunting guns have changed dramatically. When purchasing a duck gun, consider the following:

GAUGE. The lead-shot ban has led to the demise of 16- and 20-gauge guns for duck hunting. These bores simply do not deliver enough of the lighter steel shot for a clean kill at normal duck-shooting distances. Today, the 12-gauge is the choice of the great majority of duck hunters, although some prefer a 10-gauge for extra long-range killing power.

CHAMBER LENGTH. The length of your gun's chamber determines the length of the shells you can shoot. The standard chamber length in a 12-gauge is 2¾ inches; in a 10-gauge, 3 inches. Most 12-gauge magnums have a 3-inch chamber; a few, 3½. A 10-gauge magnum has a 3½-inch chamber. A standard chamber is adequate for the majority of duck hunting, although a magnum gives you about 10 percent more range. Never try to shoot a shell longer than the chamber length of your gun, which is usually stamped somewhere on the barrel.

BARREL LENGTH. Old-time duck hunters maintained that a longer barrel produced higher shot velocity, resulting in greater effective killing range. It's true that a long barrel works best for long passing shots, but not because of significantly higher shot velocity. The extra barrel length gives you a longer sighting plane, and the extra weight results in a smoother swing. For pass-shooting or any other type of hunting that requires great accuracy, select a gun with a 30- to 32-inch barrel. For jump-shooting or any other type of hunting that requires quick shots, a 22- to 26-inch barrel is a better choice because you can shoulder it and swing it in a hurry.

ACTION. Pump and semi-automatic actions are popular in duck hunting, because they enable you to fire three shots (the legal maximum under federal law) in rapid succession. The extra shots are often needed not only for multiple kills, but to finish off cripples before they can escape. Most pumps and semi-automatics have a 5-shot magazine, so they must have a plug to prevent inserting more than 3 shells.

Many hunters believe they can shoot better with a semi-automatic, because it has less recoil and no arm

SEMI-AUTOMATIC. Each pull of the trigger fires one shell, and another is automatically chambered. There are two basic types of semi-automatics: gas-operated and recoil-operated. The recoil type is very reliable, but tends to "kick" more. If you're using light loads, a recoil gun may not eject empty shells as well as a gas gun.

PUMP. Sliding the fore-end back and forth ejects a spent shell and chambers another one. With a little practice, you can shoot a pump just as fast and accurately as a semi-automatic.

DOUBLE-BARREL. To open the hinge action to insert or eject shells, you push a lever or button at the rear of the receiver. Double-barrels come in side-by-side or over-and-under models. A double has one big advantage over other actions: it gives you the option of selecting a different choke for each barrel.

movement is necessary to eject shells. But a pump is more reliable; it has fewer moving parts to malfunction in the frigid weather duck hunters often encounter. Despite the obvious advantages of a repeater, many hunters prefer double-barrels for their simplicity and the tradition that they represent.

CHOKE. To prevent the shot from scattering too much, shotgun barrels must decrease in diameter at the muzzle. The amount of constriction, called the *choke*, determines the size and density of your shot pattern.

Open (wide) chokes, such as skeet and cylinder, are seldom used for duck hunting because they do not provide shot density adequate to kill a good-sized duck at normal shooting distances. Chokes most commonly used in duck hunting (from widest to narrowest) include: improved-cylinder, modified, improved-modified and full.

As a rule, the greater the expected shooting distance, the narrower the choke you should use. But when using a full-choke barrel, shot size is also a consideration. Most shotgun manufacturers advise against using steel shot larger than size 1 because abrasion from the hard shot may "blow out" the choke. Shooting large steel shot through a full choke may result in overconstriction and too many "fliers," pellets that sail erratically and separate from the main shot group.

To determine if your choke is functioning as it should, pattern your gun. Place a bull's-eye on a large piece of paper, hang the paper in a safe spot, stand back 40 yards and shoot at the bull's-eye. Then check the target; the bull's-eye should be in the center of the pattern. If it isn't, have a gunsmith check your gun.

Next, draw a 30-inch circle around the center of the densest part of the pattern and count the number of pellet holes inside the circle. Divide this number by the number of pellets in the load and multiply by 100 to determine the percentage of shot in the circle. For an improved-cylinder, the percentage of shot in the circle at 40 yards should be in the low 40s; for a modified, the low 50s; for an improved-modified, about 60; and for a full, about 70.

Check the pattern to make sure the shot are distributed fairly evenly, with no big holes (areas with no pellet marks). Holes contribute to crippling and may even allow ducks to fly through the pattern. If there are holes, your choke is either too loose or too tight, causing too much pellet deformation.

If your choke is too tight, a gunsmith can bore it out. If it's too loose, consider installing a screw-in choke system. Screw-in choke tubes enable you to change chokes in seconds. A gunsmith should determine whether or not the system is suitable for an older gun.

Shotgun Shells

With a ban on lead shot for waterfowl hunting in effect or imminent throughout the United States and Canada, shotshell selection has become a lot more complicated. Shell manufacturers now offer a wide selection of nontoxic loads.

SHOT TYPES. The great majority of duck hunters now use steel shot, but some are opting for heavier materials such as bismuth or tungsten. Each of these materials results in a slightly different shotshell performance.

•*Steel*. Because steel is about 30 percent lighter than lead, a steel pellet does not pack the punch of a lead pellet of the same size. Air resistance causes it to lose velocity and energy more quickly. To compensate for the energy reduction, you must use shot two or three sizes larger. If you previously used size 4 lead shot, for instance, select size 1 or 2 steel shot.

The larger shot means fewer pellets in a load of the same weight. A shell loaded with 1¼ ounces of size 4 lead shot, for instance, carries 169 pellets. An equivalent load of size 2 steel, 156 pellets; size 1 steel, 129 pellets.

But steel shot has another property that helps offset its lighter weight: it is considerably harder than lead. It does not deform as much, so there are fewer fliers and the shot pattern holds together better. Even though there are fewer pellets in an equivalent load, a higher percentage of those pellets hit the target. Many veteran duck hunters who vehemently opposed steel shot are now having good success with it on waterfowl.

Components of a Steel Shotshell

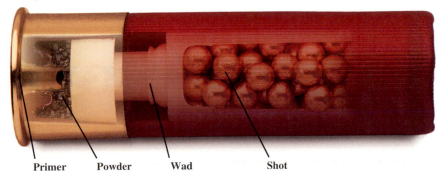

Primer   Powder   Wad   Shot

The hardness of steel shot, however, may damage your choke (p. 51). This explains why many water-fowlers refuse to shoot steel shot in their fine, thin-walled double-barrels.

•*Bismuth.* Bismuth shot has properties somewhere between those of lead and steel. It is only 10 percent lighter than lead. Because it is considerably harder and more brittle than lead, there have been some problems with the shot shattering. For performance equivalent to that of lead, you must select shot one size larger, instead of two or three sizes larger, as you would with steel. The major drawback to bismuth is its cost. A box of bismuth shells sells for about double the price of steel.

•*Tungsten-Iron.* With a weight only 6 percent less than that of lead shot, tungsten-iron shot offers performance very similar to that of lead. It is not as brittle as bismuth shot, so patterns tend to hold together better. But like bismuth shells, tungsten-iron shells are about double the price of steel.

LOADS. Compared to most upland birds, ducks are hard to kill. Their dense feathers and thick skin resist shot penetration. Consequently, the majority of duck hunters use high-power or magnum loads.

A high-power (standard load) 12-gauge, 2¾-inch shell usually contains 1⅛ ounces of steel shot; a magnum shell of the same length, 1¼ ounces. A 12-gauge, 3-inch magnum shell has 1⅜ ounces; a 3½-inch, 1⁹⁄₁₆ ounces.

Although the heavier loads give you more pellets and a denser shot pattern, they generally are somewhat slower. For instance, a standard 2¾-inch load has a muzzle velocity of about 1370 feet per second; a magnum 2¾-inch load, only 1275. The slower speed means you'll have to slightly increase your lead. To compensate for the loss of speed, some ammunition manufacturers are now making 3- and 3½-inch magnum, high-velocity loads, which contain less shot. These loads may attain a muzzle velocity of 1450 feet per second.

Many experienced duck hunters swear by standard loads, maintaining that the critical element is shot placement, not pellet count.

SHOT SIZE. The table below provides guidelines for selecting the right steel shot, depending on duck size and shooting distance.

In addition to the shells recommended for wing-shooting, duck hunters should also carry a few slapper loads. Used for killing ducks you have crippled, slapper loads contain size 6 shot. Ducks swimming away from you are notoriously hard to kill, because the only vulnerable spot is the head. The small shot give you a denser pattern, boosting your odds of a head shot.

Shot-selection Chart

SHOOTING RANGE	STEEL SHOT SIZE			MINIMUM SHOT WEIGHT
	Large ducks	Med. ducks	Small ducks	
Under 35 yards	2	3	4	¾ oz. plus
35-45 yards	BB	1 2	3	1 oz. plus
45 yards	BB	1	1	1⅛ oz. plus

Shooting

Ducks offer the ultimate wingshooting challenge. When asked how to lead a duck, a veteran waterfowler offered this simple advice: "Swing like hell!"

If duck hunters would only follow his suggestion, they would definitely bag more birds. Studies have shown that the majority of misses result from shooting behind the duck, rather than ahead of it. This is easy to understand when you consider that ducks fly about half again as fast as most upland game birds.

Not only are ducks swifter targets, duck hunters must contend with many other challenges not often faced by upland bird hunters. They are often required to shoot from a sitting position or while lying flat on their back. They may have to shoot with their feet stuck in

the mud or when weeds or brush make a smooth swing impossible. The dim light and inclement weather in which ducks fly best doesn't help your shooting either, especially when you're wearing a bulky winter parka.

Hunters accustomed to shooting lead shot may have trouble adapting to steel. Because steel is not as dense as lead, it is more easily blown off course, meaning that you have to compensate for the wind more than you would with lead. And the lower density means a shorter effective range. But steel forms tighter patterns with fewer fliers, partially compensating for the lower density.

Most upland-bird hunting involves straightaway, rising or crossing shots, but duck hunters are often faced with head-on, over-the-shoulder and descending shots, as well. When practicing, be sure to work on shots similar to those you will face in the duck blind. On the pages that follow are the most important shooting techniques and specific shots to perfect.

The best way to polish your duck-shooting skills is to do a lot of duck hunting. Short of that, do a lot of trap shooting or spend some time shooting sporting clays.

How to Shoot from Various Positions

FLAT ON YOUR BACK. When field hunting or hunting from a low-profile boat (p. 75), you may have to lie flat on your back or use a layout board (shown) to stay hidden. When the birds are in range, lean forward enough to get into a comfortable shooting position.

KNEELING. When hunting from a shore blind or field blind, you may want to kneel to keep a lower profile. But many hunters feel shaky when shooting from a kneeling position. For extra stability, try sitting on the heels of your boots.

SITTING. If you're hunting in a small boat or blind, you may be shooting from a sitting position where little hip rotation is possible. If you're right-handed, it's difficult to swing your gun to the right, because your arms won't move that way. The best solution: pivot your entire body to the right.

STANDING. This widely used position is one of the easiest to master, but if your feet are bogged down in the muck, you'll have trouble swinging on crossing ducks. Try to loosen your feet and reposition yourself so you're facing any incoming birds.

HEAD-ON. This is the shot duck hunters wait for, because you don't have to lead the bird and its vitals are completely exposed. Just put the bead on the duck's bill and pull the trigger.

CROSSING (swing-through method). To prevent shooting behind the bird, start the bead behind it and smoothly swing the gun until the bead just passes the bill. Then, shoot while continuing the swing.

LONG DISTANCE (sustained-lead method). Aim ahead of the duck and swing smoothly, maintaining a constant lead as you pull the trigger. The amount of lead, determined only by experience, depends mainly on range, flight speed and wind velocity.

OVER-THE-SHOULDER. For many hunters, this is the most difficult shot of all. Use the swing-through method, and shoot before the bird is directly overhead; otherwise, you won't be able to maintain a smooth swing.

DESCENDING. Ducks dropping into dense cover, such as flooded timber, often descend almost vertically. The tendency is to shoot over them. Be sure to aim just under the bird.

RISING. When ducks jump off the water, they seemingly suspend momentarily as they position themselves to turn with the wind. Put the bead on the bill and shoot before the bird makes this turn.

Duck-shooting Tips

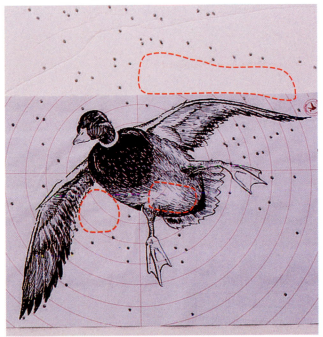

FIRE a shot into a paper target at about 40 yards, and examine the pattern. If there are noticable "holes," your choke is probably too tight. Keep trying looser chokes until your pattern evens out.

LEARN to estimate range by comparing the length of the duck with the width of your shotgun's muzzle. At 35 yards, for instance, a pintail drake is slightly wider than the muzzle (left). At 20 yards, it is twice as wide (right).

WAIT for a shot in which the vital areas (shown in red) are exposed. A head-on shot (left) gives you the best chance for a clean kill, because both wings, the head and the internal organs are exposed. Next best is a crossing shot (bottom left), which exposes one wing, the head and the internal organs. A going-away shot (below) makes a clean kill difficult; the head is hidden and the internal organs are protected by the backbone and gizzard. Shoot only if the bird is within 20 yards.

Decoys

The sight of a flock of ducks settling into the "blocks" with wings cupped and feet extended is the ultimate thrill for a waterfowler.

You can buy decoys to mimic practically any kind of common duck species, but few hunters bother getting that specific. Most puddle ducks are attracted by mallard decoys; most divers, by bluebill decoys.

One of the most common questions asked by decoy hunters is, "How many blocks do I need?" There is no easy answer, but, as a rule, the bigger the water, the more decoys are necessary to attract ducks. On a small pothole, a half-dozen decoys may be plenty, but on a huge lake, you may need a hundred or more. The best way to find out is to experiment.

But if your decoys are not set in the right place or pattern, it makes no difference how many you have; the ducks will not drop in.

In most situations, your decoys should be set on the lee side of the body of water you're hunting. Ducks prefer to set down in calm, sheltered water rather than in a windswept area with big waves. Hunters argue endlessly about the best decoy patterns, and there are no firm rules on the subject. But always remember that ducks need a clear opening to land, and would prefer not to fly over decoys to do so. They will always land into the wind, so you should leave an opening on the *downwind* side of your decoy setup. Be sure the hunters are positioned so they are in easy range of birds landing in the opening.

When you are hunting diving ducks, the birds may not land in your decoys, but they will usually follow a line of decoys that will lead them within easy gun range of your blind.

The use of *magnum* decoys has increased greatly in recent years. A standard decoy measures 15 to 16 inches long; a magnum, 18 to 20 inches. Some manufacturers even make *super-magnums,* which measure 21 inches or longer. Many hunters feel that the larger-than-normal blocks are easier for ducks to see.

Whatever decoys you use, make sure they have a realistic low-gloss finish. And don't hunt with decoys that are covered with frost or iced over. Decoys with a glossy or sparkly look are sure to spook the ducks.

Hand-carved antique decoys often command prices in the hundreds of dollars

Basic Types of Decoys

HALF-BODY FEEDER decoys simulate the rear end of a duck tipping up to feed. Some hunters scatter a few feeders among their full-body floaters to make their spread appear more realistic.

FULL-BODY FLOATING decoys may be made of wood, cork, foam or molded plastic. A weighted or water-filled keel makes them float upright, and a string and anchor keep them from drifting away. They come in standard and magnum sizes.

FIELD decoys come in full-body, shell and silhouette models. Most have a flat base or a ground stake to prevent the wind from blowing them away. The best ones extend high off the ground so the ducks can easily see them.

MOTION decoys, including shakers (top) and swimmers (bottom), have a battery-powered motor. Swimmers move in a circle; shakers make ripples. One motion decoy is enough to give life to your entire decoy spread on a calm day.

FLYING decoys are mounted on poles, which are set at the edge of your decoy spread. They simulate ducks about to join the main flock, encouraging any ducks flying over to do the same.

SLEEPER decoys are set on shore or mixed in with your floating decoys. Sleepers convey the message that "all is well."

CONFIDENCE decoys mimic gulls, herons and other water birds commonly seen around ducks. Set around the fringes of the spread, they give ducks "confidence" that the spread is real.

Decoy Materials and Design

WATER TYPES: Foam decoys (top) float very high, but are not as durable as most other types. Some models, however, have special coatings for added durability. Molded plastic decoys (middle) are durable, realistic, lightweight and inexpensive. But stray shot may puncture the hollow body, causing it to take on water. Cork decoys (bottom) are not as popular as they once were, but some still prefer them over foam models. They ride lower in the water and don't blow around as much in the wind.

FIELD TYPES: Full-body decoys (top) are extremely realistic but, because they can't be stacked, take up a lot of space. Silhouette decoys (middle) come with a stake that anchors them to the ground. They're inexpensive, compact and easy to store. Many hunters make their own, using a jigsaw. Shell decoys (bottom) stack into compact piles, enabling you to carry many decoys in a small space. Some models come with a stake that enables them to be set in shallow water.

DECOY SIZES range from standard (left), which measures 15 to 16 inches long; magnum (middle), 18 to 20 inches and super-magnum (right), 21 inches or more.

DECOY ACCESSORIES include: (1) longline clip, for attaching decoy cords to longlines; (2) snap-swivels, which attach to decoy weights to prevent cord twist; decoy weights, such as (3) mushroom anchor, (4) pyramid anchor, (5) ring anchors, (6) strap anchor and (7) scoop anchor, which slips over the decoy's bill; (8) tangle-free decoy cord; (9) braided-nylon decoy cord; (10) decoy touch-up paint and (11) grapple anchor for longlines.

DECOY BAGS are usually made of nylon mesh and have back straps which enable you to carry the bag over your shoulders.

DECOY PAINT restores the color of well-used blocks. You can buy a paint set that includes every color you need.

FLAGGING DEVICES attract the attention of ducks at a distance. Use a black flag for divers; a white or gray for puddlers.

Dog-Proof Decoy Lines

One of the biggest hassles in duck hunting is setting out large numbers of decoys. For many years, hunters have tried to save time by setting out lines of decoys, rather than singles. But retrieving dogs tend to get tangled in the cords, and if they aren't untangled quickly, they may drown. The cords also pose a constant threat to boat propellers. Here's how to rig your decoys on a weighted line that will not catch dogs or props.

MAKE a weighted decoy line using 40 to 50 feet of hard-braid nylon cord in 3/16- or 7/32-inch diameter. Make individual 3-foot lines for each decoy, using the same kind of cord; attach a large clip (inset) to one end, and tie the other end to the decoy using a loop knot or a keel knot (below). Tie a 1- to 3-pound weight, such as a grapple anchor, to each end of the line. Each line should have from 12 to 18 decoys, depending on how tight a spread you want. Because the line is submerged, it cannot catch a swimming dog or tangle in a boat propeller.

Knots for Rigging Decoys

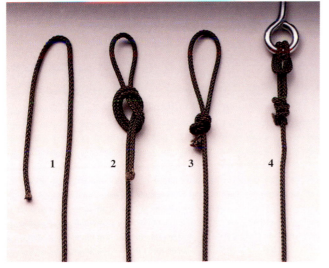

LOOP KNOT. (1) Double the line, (2) tie an overhand knot, (3) snug up the knot and burn the end and (4) attach the line to the keel eye by passing the free end through the loop. This knot makes it easy to change lines for different water depths.

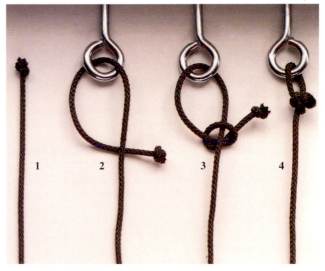

KEEL KNOT. (1) Tie an overhand knot in the end of the line or burn the end, (2) pass the cord through the keel eye, (3) tie an overhand knot around the standing line and (4) pull on the standing line to snug up the knot. This knot makes a permanent connection.

Commercial boat blind covered with camo material

Blinds

A duck's visual acuity means that you must hunt from a blind that not only conceals you, but blends in well with your surroundings. Consequently, the best blinds are made from natural materials gathered on site.

If the natural cover is high enough and dense enough, you don't need to construct a blind. Simply hide in the cover and don't move or look up at the ducks as they fly over.

Permanent blinds offer greater comfort than temporary ones, but have one major drawback. Unless you have several permanent blinds at different locations on a body of water, you have little chance of being in the best spot for the existing conditions. Another drawback: constructing and maintaining a permanent blind is a lot of work.

Many hunters mistakenly assume that they must be completely hidden to avoid detection by ducks, so they use blinds made from solid material. In reality, a blind must only break up your outline. Light camo netting, for instance, is usually sufficient to obscure

your profile. See-through material gives you the advantage of being able to watch approaching birds and read their body language.

Even the best blind, however, is of no value unless it is set in the right location. Remember, ducks will land where they want to land, not where you want them to land.

Ducks usually have a reason for landing in a particular spot. They could be feeding on a bed of submerged vegetation, resting along the lee shore to get out of the wind or rafting up in open water for the safety it provides. No matter what the reason, it is unlikely that you can do anything to change their mind. So before you choose a blind site, spend some time watching the ducks to pattern their daily movements.

Ducks on a particular body of water change location frequently as the wind switches, the food supply is exhausted or hunting pressure increases. The most successful hunters are mobile, moving whenever the ducks do. They use natural blinds or carry portable ones that transport easily and set up quickly.

Blinds are much more important for puddle ducks than for divers. You can be out in the open as a flock of divers approaches, and, if you remain still, they probably won't notice you.

Types of Natural Blinds

EMERGENT VEGETATION. Tall cattails, bulrushes or cane provide enough cover to hide a hunter or even a camouflaged boat. As the cover gets broken down, move to a new blind site.

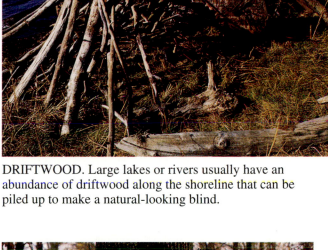

DRIFTWOOD. Large lakes or rivers usually have an abundance of driftwood along the shoreline that can be piled up to make a natural-looking blind.

SHORELINE WILLOWS. If there are willows growing along the shoreline of your hunting area, boughs can be cut and stuck in the mud to make a portable, natural-looking blind.

FLOODED TIMBER. Commonly found in reservoirs and river backwaters, standing flooded trees provide good concealment for hunters. As ducks approach, hunters may have to move to keep the trees between them and the birds.

FENCELINES. Brushy or weedy cover along fencelines makes an excellent blind for field hunters or pass-shooters.

BOULDERS. Rocky shorelines may have little in the way of vegetative cover, so hunters commonly wear dark clothing, sit among the rocks and remain motionless.

COFFIN BLIND. Usually made of fiberglass and designed for one hunter, a coffin blind has a very low profile. The blind has a backrest that enables the hunter to lean back and stay low. It is staked on both sides for stability (inset).

CAMO MESH. See-through camo mesh or even a cotton fishnet breaks up your outline enough to fool the ducks. You can drape the mesh over poles in your boat or over weeds or brush to make a ground blind.

HOMEMADE BOAT BLIND. You can custom-fit a blind to your boat by cutting chicken wire to fit around the perimeter and weaving in cane or other vegetation. Support poles every few feet fit into receptacles on the boat. You can make a land blind in much the same way. Simply carry the blind with you and push the poles into the mud.

COLLAPSIBLE LAND BLIND. This one-man blind conceals you completely. It has a seat and a window for watching the birds. When they're close enough, you step on a pedal to collapse the blind, giving you a clear shot.

COLLAPSIBLE BOAT BLIND. Designed to fit over a jon boat, this blind completely covers hunters in the boat (left). Then, when the ducks are within shooting range, a lever is pushed to drop the blind and give the hunters a clear shot (right).

MAGNUM DECOY BLIND. Blend in with your decoy spread by hiding under a giant goose decoy. Several slots are cut to view incoming ducks.

Types of Permanent Blinds

BOATHOUSE BLIND. Designed to conceal an entire boat and hunters, this blind is built around heavy posts that are driven into the ground. An opening on one end allows the boat to slip in and out easily to retrieve downed birds. A door inside the blind (not shown) enables hunters to crawl onto an attached hunting platform.

PIT BLIND. Used mainly in field hunting, a pit blind may simply be a hole in the ground deep enough to conceal a hunter who is sitting, standing or lying flat on his back. You can also dig in an upright barrel or section of culvert in which a single hunter can stand.

BOX BLIND. These blinds usually have a wooden floor and bench seats and are built around corner posts driven into the ground. They are covered with vegetation woven into chicken wire. Those with a high back are called *piano blinds*.

STILT BLIND. Used mainly in hunting divers or sea ducks, stilt blinds are much like box blinds, but are set in water as deep as 5 feet.

Duck Calls & Calling

Some accomplished duck callers attribute their success to spending countless hours on a marsh, listening to the ducks. Then, they spend a great deal more time practicing to emulate the precise sounds that the ducks make. While such precision may help win a duck-calling contest, it is seldom necessary to attract ducks. You should be able to call well enough to bring in some birds with a few hours of practice.

Practically all puddle ducks are attracted by the "quack" of the hen mallard. Hen pintails, gadwalls, teal, shovelers, black ducks and mottled ducks all make some sort of quacking sound. And even many ducks that don't quack feel comfortable in the company of mallards. Consequently, the majority of duck hunters use only a mallard call. Diving-duck hunters may use a diver call to make a purring sound, but the same sound can easily be made by rolling your tongue while blowing your mallard call.

The first step to successful calling is buying the right call. But a more expensive call is not necessarily a better one; some handmade calls retail for hundreds of dollars. Consult an experienced local duck hunter to determine what kind of call works best in your

area. The sound of a particular call may be more effective in one region than in another.

There are two basic types of mallard calls: standard, or Reelfoot style, and Arkansas style. Reelfoot calls have a metal reed that is curved upward at the tip. Arkansas calls have a straight plastic reed. Reelfoot calls are generally harder to blow and have a narrower range of tones, but are much louder.

Mallard calls are sometime categorized by their tolerance level. A low-tolerance call is easy to blow, but gives you very little volume control. If you blow too hard, it will break, meaning that the reed stops vibrating. A high-tolerance call requires more skill, but can produce a wide range of volumes, depending on the amount of air blown through it. Unlike a low-tolerance call, it will not break when you blow hard. Arkansas calls may be high or low tolerance; Reelfoot calls are always high tolerance.

Some calls have what amounts to a screw-in choke system. By switching choke tubes, you can increase or decrease the call's volume.

Besides the hen mallard call, other popular calls include:

•Wood-duck call – Makes a high-pitched "whoo-eek" squeal.

- Whistle call – Imitates the sound of a drake pintail, wigeon or teal.

- Shaker call – Makes a feeding chuckle when shaken rapidly.

- Drake mallard call – Makes a soft, raspy quack.

- Diver call – Makes the typical diver purr.

Practice calling at home or in your car, not on the duck marsh. Poor calling is the quickest way to keep birds out of your decoys. Listen to some duck-calling tapes or watch a calling video to get an idea of what various calls should sound like.

But knowing how to call is only part of the challenge. You must also know how frequently and how loudly to call. On some days, lots of calling works best; on others, it's better not to call at all. The only way to know is through experience and learning to read the ducks' body language as they react to the call.

TYPES OF DUCK CALLS include (1) diver call, (2) mallard drake call, (3) hand-crafted Reelfoot Lake mallard call (metal reed), (4) hand-crafted single-reed mallard call, (5) hand-crafted double-reed mallard call, (6) Volochoke call, (7) wood duck calls, (8) pintail-widgeon-teal whistle, (9) Arkansas-style mallard calls, (10) shaker call, which imitates mallard chuckle (inset).

LANYARDS for holding duck calls come in a variety of styles. Some hold a single call; others, up to six. The calls are secured with a spring device or a noose system (bottom lanyard).

Anatomy of a Duck Call

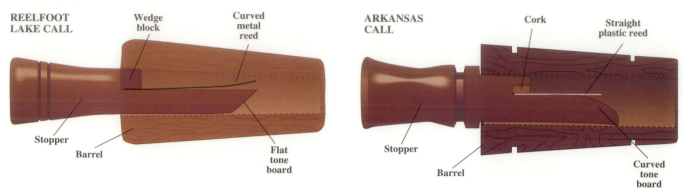

REELFOOT LAKE CALL
Wedge block — Curved metal reed
Stopper — Barrel — Flat tone board

ARKANSAS CALL
Cork — Straight plastic reed
Stopper — Barrel — Curved tone board

How to Use a Duck Call

HOLD the stopper between your thumb and forefinger.

PLACE the top of the barrel against your upper lip.

MAKE realistic single quacks by closing your hand around the stopper and then open it after starting to blow to produce a qua-**ack.**

Duck-calling Tips

CLEAN your call by pulling it apart and running cold water between the reed and tone board (left.) In the field, blow the call backward to clear any obstructions (right).

USE a double lanyard on one call to prevent losing the stopper.

AVOID calling with a glove on your hand. The fabric changes the sound of the call.

Calling All Ducks

The repertoire of a champion duck caller may include a dozen or more different calls. But for the majority of hunting situations, you need to know only four: The hail call, the greeting call, the feeding call and the comeback call. Each of these calls is described below, along with a call diagram that indicates intensity (color of type) and duration (spacing of type) of individual notes.

•HAIL CALL. Also called the *highball,* the hail call is intended to get the attention of a flock of ducks, assuming they're close enough to hear it. Point your call right at the ducks and make a series of 8 to 15 loud, pleading quacks followed by about half that many quacks of descending volume and duration.

After one or two hail calls, watch the ducks to see how they react. If they bank toward you or their wingbeat slows to a flutter, you've got their attention and no more hail calls are necesssary.

•GREETING CALL. Once you think the flock is coming your way, decrease the volume of your calling and don't call right into the birds' face. The idea is to make it sound like the call is coming from birds on the water.

The greeting call, which invites the incoming birds to join the flock, consists of a series of 5 to 10 quacks that decend in volume and duration, followed by a series of 2 long quacks and 2 or 3 shorter ones and ending with 1 long quack and 2 shorter ones.

The Hail Call

QUACK
QUACK
QUACK
QUACK
QUACK
QUACK
QUACK
QUACK
QUACK
QUACK
QUACK
QUACK
QUACK
QUACK

The Greeting Call

QUACK QUACK QUACK
QUACK QUACK QUACK
QUACK QUACK QUACK
QUACK QUACK
QUACK QUACK
QUACK
QUACK
QUACK

The Feeding Call

TICKA
TICKA
TICKA
TICKA
TICKA
TICKA
QUACK
TICKA
TICKA
TICKA
TICKA
QUACK
TICKA
TICKA
TICKA

•FEEDING CALL. This call is intended to mimic the sound made by a flock of feeding mallards. Also called the *feeding chuckle,* it is one of the most difficult calls to master. Use the feeding call when it appears that the ducks are committed to the decoys.

To make the feeding chuckle, blow into the call and say "ticka-ticka-ticka-ticka-ticka-ticka,"pausing occasionally to insert a low-volume quack. The secret to making the right sound is to rapidly flick your tongue up and down.

The feeding chuckle is easier to make with some mallard calls than it is with others. As a rule, calls that require little air flow to produce a sound work best. Arkansas calls with a double reed are very easy to blow, so they're ideal for making the feeding call. Ask a local expert, or experiment with several calls, or to find the right one, you may want to use a different call for the hail call and greeting call.

•COMEBACK CALL. Use this call if it appears that the ducks are going to fly away or land out of gun range.

The call is similar to the greeting call, but the individual quacks are louder and faster, and the overall duration of the call is longer.

When done properly, this call may convince a flock to come back for another look. It may even tempt a flock that has landed to pick up and circle your decoys.

The Comeback Call

QUACK   QUACK
QUACK   QUACK
QUACK   QUACK
QUACK   QUACK
QUACK   QUACK
QUACK   QUACK
QUACK
QUACK
QUACK
QUACK

OTHER TYPES OF CALLS. Accomplished duck callers use several other calls in addition to those already mentioned. The *lonesome hen* call, for instance, consists of 2 or 3 low-volume, drawn-out quacks, and encourages circling birds to land. The *contented mallard* call, intended to convince close-in birds that all is well, is made by blowing 1 long, high-pitched quack followed by 2 or 3 shorter, lower-pitched quacks.

Duck Boats

There are as many kinds of duck boats as there are duck habitats. Unfortunately, no single boat can be used for all hunting situations. Many serious duck hunters own several different boats for different types of hunting.

Some hunting techniques require more than one type of boat. In big-water hunting, for instance, a good-sized semi-V is often used to haul gear to the hunting area, while the hunting is done from a smaller, lower-profile craft.

One of the most common mistakes in duck hunting is using a boat that is too small for the conditions. Small boats are inexpensive, lightweight and easy to conceal, but if the water gets rough, you could pay with your life.

No matter what boat you use, it should be camouflaged to match the natural cover. Following are the most popular boat types:

CANOE. Canoes are quiet and easy to maneuver, but lack the stability needed for hunting in open water. Because they draw very little water, they work well for float-hunting (p. 126) and hunting in small, shallow sloughs. Canoes also come in handy for hauling gear when wading. Square-stern canoes can be outfitted with a small outboard motor. Canoes are usually made of aluminum or fiberglass.

PIROGUE. Similar to a canoe, a pirogue is a traditional craft used mainly by southern duck hunters. A pirogue differs from a canoe in that it has a flatter bottom and shorter sides with a wider flare. The pirogue's popularity stems from its ability to traverse the shallow water and narrow passages found in bayous and flooded timber. Generally made of fiberglass, these lightweight boats weigh only 40 to 60 pounds.

JON BOAT. Among the most popular duck-hunting craft, these flat-bottomed boats are very stable and have a low profile. But the square bow makes them a poor choice for rough water or pushing through heavy vegetation. Some jon boats have a semi-V bow, so they part the waves and weeds much better. Most jon boats are made of aluminum.

SEMI-V. The term "semi-V" describes a boat with a V-shaped hull at the bow that gradually flattens toward the stern. Large semi-Vs, 16- to 20-footers with 20- to 60-hp motors, are ideal for transporting equipment, hunters and dogs to the hunting site, especially on big water. You can easily hunt from a 12- to 14-foot semi-V, with many hunters attaching their blind directly to the boat. Most semi-Vs used for duck hunting are made of aluminum.

POKE BOAT. Made of wood or fiberglass, these kayak-like boats have a low profile and are pointed at each end, so they slide easily through vegetation and can be poked into available cover instead of using a blind. Wider and more stable than a canoe, they can be used for most types of duck hunting.

FLOAT TUBE. Also called a belly boat, a float tube consists of a nylon-covered inner tube with a built-in seat. The hunter wears neoprene waders, sits in the seat and propels himself with kick fins. Float tubes work well for hunting potholes too deep for wading, float-hunting, setting and picking up decoys and retrieving birds. They are not recommended for hunting in cover that could cause a puncture.

KICK BOAT. This small personal watercraft has a seat between a pair of pontoons. It can be propelled with either kick fins or oars. Kick boats are more stable than float tubes, and can be used in bigger water. They have a cargo rack in the rear for carrying decoys or other equipment. Unlike float tubes, kick boats keep most of your body out of the water, keeping you warmer.

LAYOUT BOAT. Used primarily on big water, these wood or fiberglass boats have an extremely low profile, making it possible to hunt without a blind. The wide hull has an elevated cowling that keeps the hunters from getting wet while they're lying down and looking up at the birds. Because layout boats are normally used in open water, they are often painted black for minimum visibility. They are usually towed to the hunting site with a large boat and then anchored amid the decoys with the bow into the wind.

SCULLING BOAT. Also similar to a layout boat, a sculling boat is propelled by a curved oar that extends out a hole in the transom. The hunter lies down in the cockpit and works the oar in a figure-8 motion to propel the boat. Sculling boats are normally used to approach rafts of ducks in calm, open water. Hunters often drive along the shore until they spot a raft of birds; then they launch the boat and scull out to within shooting range.

SNEAK BOAT. Similar to a layout boat, a sneak boat is designed for one or two hunters who sit on the floor while the boat drifts into a flock of ducks in open water. A hinged canopy on the bow keeps the hunters hidden. Another boat tows the sneak boat to the hunting area, and, after the decoys are set, the hunters paddle about 200 yards upwind and wait for a flock of ducks to land in the blocks before starting their drift. When they get close enough, they push down the canopy to give them a clear shot.

LABRADOR RETRIEVER. By far the most popular of all waterfowl dogs, the *lab* will not hesitate to jump into icy water and stay in it for long periods to retrieve downed birds. Labs also excel at retrieving on land and make very good upland bird dogs. The lab's smooth, short, burr-proof coat may be black, yellow (top inset) or chocolate (bottom inset). Labs average about 65 pounds, although some may weigh more than 100.

Dogs for Duck Hunting

ew avid duck hunters would think of going afield without a good retrieving dog. Not only is it tremendously satisfying to see a well-trained retriever do his job, you'll wind up with considerably more ducks in your bag at the end of the day.

Studies conducted by the U.S. Fish and Wildlife Service have shown that about one out of every four ducks downed by hunters is not recovered. Many experienced duck hunters place the losses even higher. A good retriever will greatly reduce your loss ratio, making you feel better about your hunt and contributing toward improved waterfowl conservation.

Practically any mutt with the instinct to retrieve can be used to fetch ducks. But only a few breeds are recommended for use in the icy, rough water that duck hunters must often contend with. The Labrador, Chesapeake and golden retrievers are, by far, the most popular waterfowling breeds, although some hunters use other retrievers, such as the curly-coated retriever and American water spaniel. The German wire-haired pointer makes a very good combination waterfowl-upland dog.

It pays to buy a dog from a reputable breeder. You could probably get one cheaper from a friend or by looking in the newspaper, but you'd have no guarantee of strong hunting bloodlines. And should the dog develop health problems, such as hip displasia, a reputable breeder will usually replace it.

In waterfowl hunting, a poorly trained dog is worse than no dog at all. It may jump in the water as ducks approach your blind, spoiling your shooting. Or it may move suddenly as the birds swing overhead, alerting them to your presence. If it does swim after a downed bird, it may not bring it back to you.

You can probably do the basic obedience training yourself. Most young dogs are quick to learn the basic commands: come, sit, heel, kennel and fetch. But unless you've had some retriever-training experience, leave the advanced training to a professional. Hand signals, blind retrieves and multiple retrieves are much more difficult for a dog to learn, but an experienced trainer knows the tricks that will simplify the process.

GOLDEN RETRIEVER. An excellent water dog with equally good upland skills, the affectionate golden retriever has a "softer" temperament than the Labrador or Chesapeake. Goldens average 65 pounds.

CHESAPEAKE BAY RETRIEVER. Although "chessies" tend to be independent, hard-to-train dogs, they are regarded as the hardiest cold-weather, rough-water breed. These dogs average 70 pounds.

GERMAN WIRE-HAIRED POINTER. Also called the Draathar, this breed has a thick, wiry, water-repellent coat and is as good a waterfowl retriever as it is an upland bird dog. Draathars average 60 pounds.

Clothing

Every veteran duck hunter has seen it happen: the day starts out cold and blustery, but, by early afternoon, the mercury has climbed 30 degrees and you're swatting mosquitoes. The best way to deal with this problem is to develop a layering system that allows you to take off or add clothing as the weather changes.

The type of clothing you need depends on the type of hunting you'll be doing and where you're doing it. You may need each of the following items or only a few of them.

PARKA. A must for cold-weather hunting, a parka is generally worn with insulated, bib-style pants. Be sure your parka fits loosely enough so you can wear it over lighter clothing, such as a hooded sweatshirt, yet easily swing your gun. Here are some things to keep in mind when selecting a parka:

•Durability – The shell should be made of tough, long-lasting material such as tightly woven nylon.

•Camouflage – Select the camo pattern that best matches the cover in which you'll be hunting. Some coats are reversible, giving you the option of two different camo patterns.

•Water Repellency – The shell should be waterproof or have a breathable waterproof liner to protect you against rain, snow or splashing waves. Breathable shells are more expensive, but prevent perspiration buildup.

Parka with zip-out liner

•Liner – Many parkas come with a zip-out liner that can be quickly removed for hunting in warm weather. Or, you can wear the liner but not the shell. This adds great versatility to your hunting outfit.

•Pockets – A good parka has plenty of pockets for shells, gloves, extra calls and other accessories.

WADING JACKET. If you'll be hunting in waders, you need a jacket short enough that it won't get wet. An elastic band along the bottom helps keep the jacket snug at the waist to prevent a draft. A wading jacket should have the same features as a good parka.

PANTS. Available in insulated or uninsulated models, water-

Wading jacket

fowling pants usually have a tough nylon camo shell and a liner of Gore-Tex® or other breathable material. Some hunters prefer pants to bibs, because they're less bulky and more comfortable. But they may not be warm enough in very cold weather. Some lightweight pants can be worn inside waders.

Waterfowling pants

BIBS. If you're not using waders, you'll want insulated, waterproof camo bibs that extend up to chest level. Be sure the legs have zippers long enough that you can easily slip the bibs over your boots. In mild weather, you can wear bibs with only a camo shirt; in cold weather, under a parka. Bibs are usually made from the same materials as parkas.

Bibs should slip easily over boots

FOOTWEAR for duck hunting includes: (1) neoprene waders, which come in 3mm, 4mm or 5mm thicknesses, for warm-, cool- or cold-weather hunting (you can also buy rubber waders, which are less expensive, and fabric-coated rubber waders, in which the rubber is sandwiched between two layers of canvas or Cordura®, for extra durability); (2) hip boots, which also come in fabric-coated rubber (shown), neoprene and rubber models; (3) leather boots, for warm-weather hunting on dry land and (4) felt-lined pac boots, for late-season, cold-weather hunting.

WADERS/HIP BOOTS/OTHER BOOTS.

Waders or hip boots are a necessity for most types of duck hunting. Even if you're hunting on land, they'll keep you from getting wet and muddy. Be sure they fit tightly at the ankle; otherwise, they'll pull off easily when you're walking in muck.

A pair of rubber hip boots comes in handy for setting decoys in shallow water or hunting flooded fields. But for deeper water, you'll need waders. Neoprene waders are quickly gaining in popularity on the more traditional rubber or fabric-coated-rubber types. They are warmer and more comfortable than the others, but are more expensive and not quite as durable. Most duck hunters prefer boot-foot to stocking-foot waders, because the shoes that fit over the latter type tend to fill with mud and debris. Always wear a well-tightened belt around the waist of your waders. This way, they won't completely fill with water should you wade too deep or fall in.

In very cold weather, when much of the water has frozen up, felt pacs make the best footwear. The rubber bottoms allow you to walk in some water and the thick insulation keeps your feet warm even when you're sitting in a blind for hours.

GLOVES/MITTS.

For picking up decoys or doing other work on the water, you'll want waterproof gloves. Rubber gloves will do the job, but they're very stiff and won't keep your hands warm in frigid weather. Neoprene gloves are warmer and more flexible.

Neoprene gloves keep hands warm and dry

While waiting for the ducks to come, most hunters wear Gore-Tex/Thinsulate® gloves or chopper mitts, which are removed just prior to the shot. Some hunters prefer to leave their gloves on, however, so they use fingerless wool gloves or thin cotton ones.

Fingerless gloves are ideal for cold-weather shooting

CAPS/HATS. Most early-season hunters wear a camo baseball cap, with or without earflaps, or a traditional Jones-style duck-hunting cap. With either, the bill keeps the sun out of your eyes and helps reduce facial glare. As the weather worsens, switch to an insulated waterfowler's cap or, better yet, a wool or Thinsulate stocking cap. In extremely cold weather, a fur cap with earflaps is the best choice. Some hunters also wear a camo face mask, not only to help keep warm, but to allow them to look up at the birds.

UNDERWEAR/SOCKS. Long underwear and warm socks are a must for most duck hunting, but when you're slogging through mud to pick up a duck or move decoys, you'll work up a major sweat. Later, when you're sitting in the blind, the damp underlayer will make you feel cold. Polypropylene underwear and socks solve the problem. They wick moisture away from the skin so it collects in an absorbent outer layer of clothing. For that reason, many hunters wear a cotton T-shirt and long johns over their polypropylene underwear and wool socks over their polypropylene socks.

EXTRA CLOTHING. Despite your best efforts to stay dry, there will be days when your clothing will get soaked. A waterproof bag with a dry shirt, pants, underwear and socks can save the day.

Jones-style cap

Fur cap

Camo baseball cap with earflaps

Waterfowler's cap

Wool stocking cap

Face mask

Camo baseball cap

ACCESSORY BAGS, made of waterproof Cordura or nylon, can be used to carry such items as extra calls, extra shells, gloves, handheld GPS (global positioning system), first-aid kit, matches, insect repellent, screw-in chokes, gun cleaner, compact binoculars, thermos, water bottle, warm cap, hand warmers, flashlight and headlamp.

Duck-Hunting Accessories

If you're like most duck hunters, you own more waterfowling accessories than you have pockets to carry them. To keep your gear dry and well organized, consider buying a durable, waterproof accessory bag (above) that you can carry to your hunting site.

Many waterfowlers simply carry all their gear in a 5- or 6-gallon pail, which doubles as a seat. But without a lid, a pail is uncomfortable and won't keep your gear dry. Some manufacturers make camouflaged pails with padded lids (opposite) and shoulder straps. A few pails even have storage compartments.

Shown on the following pages are most of the accessories used in the sport of duck hunting. You certainly don't need all of them, but there are times when each of these items will come in handy.

HAND WARMERS. Disposable warmers can be inserted into gloves or mitts in cold weather. You can shoot much better with warm hands. Warmers are also used by callers who don't want to wear gloves because they muffle the call.

HANDHELD GPS. Big-water duck hunters often hunt in foggy weather. With a handheld GPS, you can always find your way to your blind and back again. A GPS is also helpful when hunting in vast stands of flooded timber or other continuous cover.

WATERPROOF MAT. A drab-colored tent pad or piece of canvas will keep you and your gun dry on wet ground.

MARSH STOOL. Usually made of metal, a marsh stool has a sturdy vinyl seat and duck bills (inset) that keep the stool stable and prevent it from sinking into the mud.

PLASTIC PAIL. A 5-gallon camo pail fitted with a padded seat makes a waterproof storage container for shells, gloves, lunch bags, calls, etc.

PUSH POLE. A duck-billed push pole is a must for poling your boat when the bottom is mucky. The duck bill (inset) spreads when you push but folds up as you pull, so the pole can easily be lifted out of the muck.

PLASTIC GARBAGE CAN. Enables you to carry a large number of decoys with only minor scuffing.

BINOCULARS. Used for identifying distant ducks and spotting cripples. Compact binocs are adequate in most situations, but a full-sized pair works better under low-light conditions.

SPOTTING SCOPE. Used when scouting, a spotting scope enables you to get a close look at the kind of ducks and their precise location. A car-window mount helps keep the scope stable.

GAME SLING. These devices free up your hands for carrying other gear. This model has a shoulder strap and loops that cinch down on the ducks' necks.

SHELLBOX. These waterproof cases enable you to carry several boxes of shells. Some are large enough to hold other items, such as a flashlight, binoculars, gloves and a lunch bag.

FANNY PACK. A small fanny pack works well for carrying shells, a water bottle, etc., when you're hunting in waders. Adjust the strap so the pack rests on your chest, above the waterline.

SHOTGUN SLING. A sling enables you to carry your shotgun on your shoulder, freeing up your hands so you can set decoys or carry other equipment.

CAMO TAPE. Used to cover any shiny surface of your shotgun to prevent ducks from spotting the telltale glare.

MAP BOOK. Designed specifically for sportsmen, these books contain maps of each county in a particular state. They include information valuable to duck hunters, such as location of public hunting areas and public-access sites.

Duck-Hunting Techniques

Duck-Hunting Basics

When asked to explain his consistent duck-hunting success, a veteran waterfowler offered this advice: "Hunt where the ducks want to be – not where you want to be."

To find out where the ducks want to be, you must do some preliminary scouting. Get some good topographic maps of the area you wish to hunt, along with a plat book that shows land ownership; then spend some time driving around and looking for ducks, both in the air and on the water. A good pair of binoculars will help you identify ducks at long range and spot hard-to-see birds that are swimming along shorelines or in vegetation.

Puddle ducks are most active in early morning and late in the day, so those are the best times to do your scouting. Divers, on the other hand, stay close to their feeding area, so you can scout most anytime.

While scouting, it's also important to determine the water depth. You can get a pretty good idea of how deep the water is by looking at the surrounding terrain. If the shoreline slopes very gradually or you can see clumps of vegetation visible far away from shore, chances are the water is shallow, meaning that you can hunt in hip boots or waders. If the shoreline slopes steeply, however, you'll probably need a boat. The only way to find out for sure is to put on a pair of waders and test the depth before your hunt.

If the area the ducks are using is on private land, you'll need permission to hunt. Check your plat book to see who owns the land, then politely introduce yourself and ask permission, being very specific about where you wish to hunt. Don't assume a "yes" gives you permission to hunt all season; ask each time you return.

Assuming you're granted permission, inspect the hunting area more closely to determine the best blind site for different wind conditions. It's better to figure this out in advance than to arrive in darkness on the day of the hunt and then try to figure it out.

The best blind is natural vegetation such as cattails, cane (phragmites) or willows. If there is no natural vegetation where you want to hunt, you'll have to make a blind by cutting nearby vegetation or setting up an artificial blind.

If you'll be using decoys, make sure the spot you select has enough open water to accommodate the blocks while leaving a clear landing strip. Ducks hesitate to set down in the decoys if they have to fly over other decoys to reach the landing area. Instead, they'll probably land well short of the decoys and out of gun range.

Place your blind/decoy setup where the wind is at your back, because ducks always land into the wind. Preferably, the sun should not be shining directly into your face. Direct sun not only makes it more difficult to see the ducks, it makes it easier for the ducks to see you. Whether or not you're facing into the sun, resist the urge to look up when the ducks are circling. And don't set up near other hunters or you'll both be competing for the same ducks. If you see someone in the spot you wanted to hunt, go somewhere else.

Once you have chosen your spot and started to hunt, you may find that the ducks are not flying your way. If you see flock after flock working the other end of a pothole, for instance, you have no choice but to move your setup to where the ducks are. Once the daily flight pattern has been established, it's unlikely

that it will change, unless there is a major wind shift or a change in the weather.

As a flock of ducks approaches the blind, a duck hunter's biggest dilemma is: should I shoot, or should I wait for a better shot? The answer to that question will only come with experience, as you learn to read the birds' body language. When two or more hunters share the blind, the most experienced hunter makes the decision on when to "take 'em."

When a flock of mallards is flying with a steady wingbeat, for instance, the birds probably have no intention of landing; shoot if they're in range. If they bank quickly or their wingbeat slows to a flutter, however, they've seen the decoys or heard your call; let them circle to come in closer. If the birds seem to be coming but suddenly flare, they've seen something they don't like; take them while you have a chance.

If the ducks can see into your blind when they fly over, it's important to be well camouflaged and stay motionless. If you look up at the birds as they're circling or make any sudden movement, they'll be gone in an instant.

Should you be lucky enough to set up in an area the ducks are using, don't burn out the spot. Move your blind a little every few days or, better yet, find several hunting spots on different waters so you can rest each spot for a day or two.

Judging by the number of duck hunters afield on the season opener and the sound of a typical opening-day barrage, one might think that is the only time to shoot a duck. Surveys show that the rate of harvest is, in fact, highest in early season, probably because the local ducks have not yet been "educated."

But many die-hard duck hunters prefer the late season. By that time, the vast majority of hunters have given up, so the waters are much less crowded. And with fresh birds arriving from the North, many of which have never been shot at, hunting is as good or better than it was in early season.

Be sure you know how to identify the ducks most common in your area, because most states now have species- or sex-specific bag limits that can be quite confusing. For instance, the total bag limit may be 5 ducks, with 2 wood ducks and 3 mallards, only 1 of which may be a hen mallard.

Duck-Hunting Safety

In duck hunting, as in any type of hunting, the usual safety rules apply:

•Always keep the muzzle of your shotgun pointed away from yourself and other hunters.

•Don't load your gun until you're ready to hunt, and unload it as soon as you're done.

•Make sure the safety is on until the instant you shoot.

•Never shoot in the direction of other hunters or buildings. Pellets may deflect off the water or rain down on hunters as far as 200 yards away.

•When hunting from a blind or pit, hunters should either all stand or all sit when shooting. If not, the hunters sitting could shoot the standing hunter.

•Don't lean your gun anyplace where it could fall and discharge.

•Never carry shells of different gauges in your hunting coat. If you mistakenly insert a 20-gauge shell into a 12-gauge gun, for instance, it may lodge in the barrel. Then, firing a 12-gauge shell could result in a disastrous explosion.

•Watch the weather carefully when hunting on water, and pick up well in advance of an approaching storm.

•Always carry warm clothes and a survival kit in case you are trapped by the weather.

•Never hunt when you're fatigued or your judgment has been impaired by alcohol or drugs.

•Refuse to hunt with anyone who is not cognizant of gun safety.

In addition to these basic safety rules, here are some other safety precautions for waterfowlers:

Hunter A shooting zone

Hunter B shooting zone

ESTABLISH shooting zones. With two hunters, for instance, the shooting zone is divided in half, and each hunter shoots only at birds in his shooting window. With three hunters, the window is divided into thirds. This ensures that you'll never be shooting in the direction of another hunter.

KEEP shotguns pointed out opposite ends of the boat or blind when hunting with a companion. This way, nobody is in the line of fire should a gun accidentally discharge.

SHOOT from a sitting position when hunting in a small boat or canoe. If you stand up, recoil from the shotgun blast could cause you to lose your balance and tip the boat.

CARRY a stick or wading staff when hunting in waders. The staff helps feel any dangerous drop-offs and, should you trip, helps you keep your balance.

DO NOT overload your boat with decoys or other gear; a boat riding too low in the water could easily capsize should the wind come up. If necessary, tow a separate boat to carry your gear.

DO NOT position your boat lengthwise to the shooting zone when hunting with a companion. Otherwise, one hunter has to shoot over the other's head.

WEAR a life jacket when traveling to your hunting spot in a duck boat.

CHECK the muzzle for mud or snow after a fall; a clogged muzzle could cause the barrel to explode.

AVOID hunting in a small boat with a dog. It could easily upset the boat when it plunges in to retrieve a duck. If you want to use a dog, attach a dog platform to the boat or put the dog on a nearby muskrat house.

How Weather Affects Duck Hunting

A longtime duck hunter once noted, "What's good weather for ducks is bad weather for everything else." Turns out there's a great deal of wisdom in that statement.

As a rule, hunting is best under conditions where visibility is somewhat limited. Light snow, drizzle or fog causes ducks to fly low, within easy shooting range. The limited visibility also means the birds are more likely to interpret the decoys as being the real thing. But extremely low visibility usually prevents the birds from flying at all, because they cannot see well enough to navigate.

In sunny weather, ducks tend to fly early and late in the day and sit tight during midday. But when skies are overcast, the morning and evening activity period lasts longer; when the ceiling is very low, they may fly all day long.

Another important factor is wind. The birds generally move about more in windy weather than in calm weather, and they usually fly lower, where winds are less severe. High winds move the birds off big water onto potholes, sloughs and creeks. Or, the birds may simply move to the lee side of a large lake. Of

course, wind velocity and direction also affect placement of blinds and decoys.

Ducks can sense an impending storm, so they fly to feeding areas well before the storm arrives. If the storm is severe, they sit tight until it passes and then fly back out again. So the best time to hunt may be the day before or the day after a storm, rather than the day of the storm.

The effects of weather are less pronounced in early season. The birds do not burn up as many calories in warm weather as in cold, so there is less need to fly to feeding areas when a storm approaches.

Watching the weather forecast helps hunters determine when ducks will be active. The spacing of isobars on a weather map is important. Closely spaced isobars typically signal a falling barometer accompanied by colder temperatures, precipitation and wind – conditions that cause ducks to move about and feed heavily. A strong front in Saskatchewan, for instance, may also push ducks southward, spelling good hunting in North Dakota.

Severe weather in late season may trigger a major migration. Often, the birds move just ahead of a front that is bringing in northerly winds, cold temperatures, snow, sleet or a combination of these. If the front is severe enough, up to 75 percent of the birds may leave within a 24-hour period, virtually putting an end to the season's hunting.

Good Weather for Duck Hunting

HEAVY OVERCAST often means that ducks will fly all day. Plus, the birds will have more difficulty spotting hunter movement and glare from faces and decoys.

WINDY WEATHER keeps ducks moving as they search for a calm spot to sit down. The wind also keeps them flying low.

FOG or light precipitation keeps ducks within easy shooting range. They must fly close to the ground in order to see well enough to navigate.

Bad Weather for Duck Hunting

"BLUEBIRD" WEATHER causes ducks to fly high, out of shooting range. It also helps them spot hunters and recognize decoys as fakes.

HEAVY PRECIPITATION or severe storms keep ducks sitting tight. So does dense fog or other low-visibility conditions. Flying would put them at risk for running into power lines and other obstacles.

Puddle-Duck Hunting

The widespread distribution of puddle ducks, combined with their excellent table quality, accounts for their tremendous popularity among waterfowl hunters.

As a rule, puddle ducks prefer smaller water than diving ducks; even the shallowest slough or tiniest creek may offer top-rate hunting. But puddlers are also found on some of the continent's largest waters, including the Great Lakes and Utah's Great Salt Lake. While divers are comfortable riding out big waves in open water, puddlers are usually found in calm water. In windy weather, they seek shelter along a lee shore.

You don't need a lot of expensive equipment to hunt puddle ducks. Jump-shooting and pass-shooting require nothing more than a shotgun and a few shells, and you can decoy the birds into a small body of water with only a half-dozen blocks. Hunting on big water, however, is much more involved and requires considerably more equipment, including a good-sized boat and a minimum of several dozen decoys.

Mallards are the most numerous of the puddle ducks, and most other puddler species feel comfortable in their company. Teal, for instance, are commonly seen flying with mallards, and wood ducks often loaf in the same area as mallards. As a result, you can use mallard decoys and calls to attract most any kind of puddle duck.

In setting decoys for puddle ducks, remember that puddlers rest in looser groups than divers, so your decoys can be spread out much more. Some hunters leave as much as 10 feet between individual blocks. Diving duck hunters seldom leave more than 6 feet.

Calling is of utmost importance in puddle-duck hunting. The birds, by nature, are quite vocal, and they look for reassurance from ducks on the water before making the decision to land. If you are not a competent caller, however, it's better not to call; you'll scare away more birds than you'll attract.

Puddlers are generally considered to be smarter than divers, but this "intelligence" may, in part, be a reflection of their migration and feeding habits. Because they migrate earlier than divers, they're exposed to a longer period of hunting pressure, so they're more likely to recognize the difference between decoys and the real thing.

Pothole Hunting

The secret to successful pothole hunting is finding the right pothole. Every seasoned duck hunter knows that the birds have definite preferences, often for reasons known only to them. They will flock into a certain pothole in astounding numbers, bypassing dozens of others that look nearly identical.

The best way to determine which potholes ducks are likely to use is to do some scouting. Drive through pothole country in early morning, when the ducks are moving. You may see flock after flock of ducks funneling into the same pothole.

If you must do your scouting in midday, carry binoculars and look for dark spots or movement along the shoreline and in the emergent vegetation. Study the ducks carefully to make sure they're the type you want to hunt.

When you find the right pothole, look it over to determine where there is adequate cover to set up in different wind directions. If there is little cover near the water, look for weeds or brush that could be moved into position to make a blind.

If you're hunting a small pothole, no more than 10 acres, you can probably get by with only a dozen decoys. On a bigger pothole, you may need 2 or 3 dozen. The only way to know for sure is to experiment.

Ducks respond well to decoys set properly in a pothole (pp. 98-99), so most of your shooting will be at close range. A 12-gauge pump or semi-automatic shotgun with a modified choke or an improved/modified double-barrel, along with size 3 or 4 steel shot, is ideal for the majority of pothole hunting.

Many potholes are shallow enough that you can easily hunt them with waders and walk out into the middle to retrieve downed birds. Be sure to check the depth and hardness of the bottom before hunting; you may find that you need a boat or a dog to retrieve birds and pick up decoys.

Don't attempt to hunt a very small pothole if someone else is already hunting there; you'll both be shooting at the same flocks of ducks and frustrating each other.

You can burn out a small pothole in a hurry if you hunt it frequently, especially in early season when the same local birds are working it each day. Better to rotate between potholes, letting each one rest for a few days between hunts.

Once shallow potholes begin to freeze up in late fall, the ducks move to deeper potholes or to nearby lakes and rivers that still have open water, so hunters must adjust their tactics accordingly.

How to Select a Good Pothole

IRREGULAR potholes with lots of narrow fingers are more attractive to ducks than potholes with a round, uniform shape.

POTHOLES near feeding fields draw ducks in bad weather, when they are reluctant to make long flights. On sunny days, they're willing to fly much farther to feed.

HEAVILY VEGETATED potholes, especially those with plenty of openings for ducks to land, are better than "clean" potholes. Pondweeds, coontail and other submerged plants also attract a variety of ducks.

LOW-LYING potholes nestled between hills offer protection from the wind and are more attractive to ducks than windswept potholes in flat terrain.

SECLUDED potholes away from most human activity are better for duck hunting than potholes along busy roads or near buildings. Avoid heavily hunted potholes. It takes only a few hunts to burn out a small pothole.

HUNT deep potholes or those with a bottom too soft for wading by using a kick boat or float tube with kick fins. Few potholes have a boat access, and some may even be impossible to reach with a four-wheel-drive vehicle, but these watercraft solve the problem. They are best on small waters that don't get rough.

SHORTEN your decoy string by tying a half-hitch around the keel when hunting shallow potholes. Extra string may be visible or allow the decoys to swing out of position.

WEAR a fanny pack on your chest for carrying shells when hunting a pothole in waders. This way, the shells stay dry and are easily accessible.

USE mainly dull-colored hen mallard decoys in early season. Most of the drakes are not yet fully feathered, and too many bright-colored drakes makes your decoy spread look unnatural.

PUT your dog on a muskrat house when hunting a pothole. Otherwise, the dog will either have to stay on shore or stand in the water as you hunt.

USE a retriever to fetch ducks on potholes with a mucky bottom. If you attempt to wade after them, you could get stuck and the water may top your waders.

Hunting Big-Water Puddle Ducks

If you're not bothered by the thought of towing a boat full of decoys across rough water through spitting snow at 4:30 a.m., you'll probably enjoy big-water duck hunting.

Once potholes and small lakes begin to freeze up, puddle ducks head for big water, including large lakes and river systems. Because of the huge concentrations of birds that develop, big water offers some of the year's best hunting – for waterfowlers willing to pay the price. Another good time to hunt big water is in dry years, when many small lakes and potholes have little, if any, water. Big water also collects ducks driven off of smaller lakes and potholes by heavy hunting pressure.

Primarily a mallard technique, big-water hunting may also be effective for pintails, wigeon, gadwalls and, occasionally, wood ducks. All of these species are attracted to mallard decoys and calls.

Big-water hunters hope for windy weather. On a bluebird day, the ducks may raft up in the middle of the lake or reservoir, where it's nearly impossible to get any shooting. A strong wind will keep them moving as they search for a calm spot on the lee side.

Rafts of ducks using big water generally roost in the same location each evening. They fly out to feed in early morning and then return to a shallow puddle area where they drink and dabble before heading back to the roosting area. Never attempt to hunt right in the roosting or puddle areas; gunning in these critical locations will cause the ducks to pull out. Instead, hunt the fringes of the roosting area. A little scouting may be necessary to determine the location of these spots.

A good-sized boat is a must for big-water hunting, not only to carry the hunters, but to haul the decoys, which sometimes number in the hundreds. The bigger the water, the more decoys you need to get the ducks' attention. When hunting big water, numbers of decoys are much more important than decoy size, because you are competing with such a large number of ducks.

With all the equipment required for big-water hunting, organization is extra important. Be sure to arrange your equipment neatly and avoid placing too much weight in the boat's bow. To gain space and minimize weight in their boat, some hunters carry their decoys and other equipment by towing a separate boat. If you have a choice, don't cross open water; follow the lee shoreline whenever possible, even if it makes for a longer trip.

You need a reliable shotgun, preferably a 12-gauge, that will function in frigid weather. Some automatics freeze up easily, leaving you with a single-shot. This explains why many big-water hunters use pumps or double-barrels. Since most shots will be within 35 yards, use steel shot in sizes 2 or 3.

Warm, waterproof clothing is needed, especially if you must make a long boat ride across open water. A layered parka with a down or Thinsulate liner and waterproof shell is ideal; the shell will protect you from spray on the boat ride, and you can shed it for more comfortable shooting once you reach your blind.

In most big-water hunting situations, you can hide your boat(s) in tall emergent vegetation or woody cover. But if the vegetation is sparse, you'll need a portable boat blind. Position crosswise to the decoy set if there is more than one hunter; this way, everyone has a clear shot at the birds.

As ducks approach the blind, rise slowly to get into shooting position. The birds won't see you because they're focusing on the large decoy spread. If you jump up too quickly, they'll notice the movement and flare.

Hardy retrievers, such as Chesapeakes and Labradors, are the best choice for big-water hunting. They are willing to make long retrieves in choppy water, and their heavy, water-resistant coat keeps them warm in below-freezing weather. Any dog used in big-water hunting should be trained to follow hand signals. This way, if it swims out and doesn't see the bird, it will look back at you for directions.

Before sending out your dog, however, shoot any cripples with a slapper load (size 6 steel shot). You don't want your dog chasing ducks while hunters are still shooting.

Big-water hunting has long been glorified in waterfowling literature, and it is surely one of the most productive methods. But its popularity is slowly fading as today's duck hunters opt for simpler techniques that require less time, equipment and dedication.

WIND STRAIGHT OFFSHORE (single blind). Place your decoys in the most protected area of the bay, leaving an opening about 15 yards wide for the birds to land in the middle of the spread. The opening should be directly in front of the blind. In all of these big-water spreads, the outermost decoys should be no more than 35 yards from the blind. Depending on the size of the water you're hunting, you'll need from 6 to 20 dozen decoys.

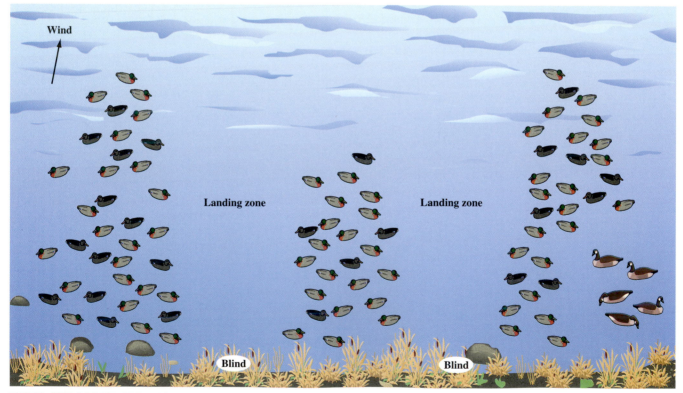

WIND STRAIGHT OFFSHORE (two blinds). When there are four or more hunters, split up and use two blinds. Follow the instructions in the diagram above, but leave two openings – one in front of each blind – instead of a single opening.

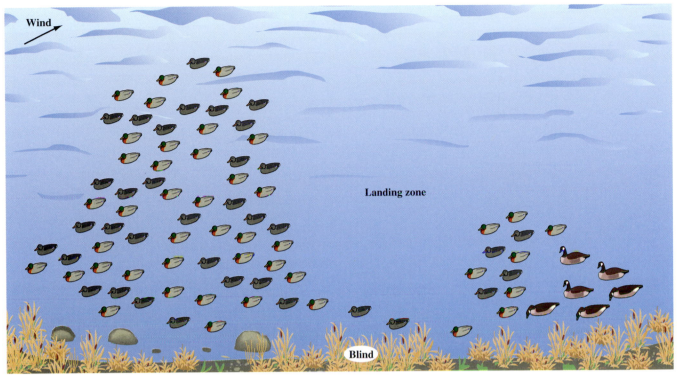

WIND ANGLING OFFSHORE. If the wind is angling from the left, leave a good-sized opening for the birds to land on the right of the decoy spread. The opening should be directly in front of the blind.

POINT SPREAD. With the wind straight offshore, set decoys in front of the point and on either side, leaving a 15-yard-wide landing spot off the tip of the point. If desired, place a few decoys on shore. The opening should be directly in front of the blind.

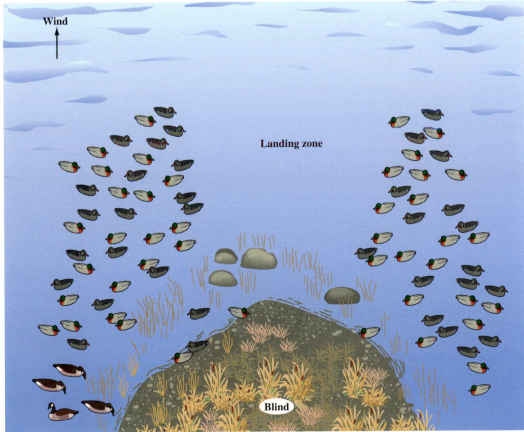

RIG your decoys on longlines (p. 63). This way, you can set and pick them up very quickly. Using about 50 feet of weighted cord, attach the decoys about 6 feet apart and tie a 1- to 3-pound weight on either end.

PULL on a string run through the eye of an anchor and attached to a decoy. Pulling the string makes the decoy dive, adding realism to your decoy spread on calm days.

SET single decoys to break up the unnatural regular pattern of a longline. To minimize tangling, do not attempt to set singles until all the longlines have been set out.

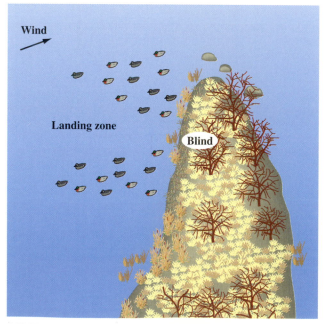

AVOID setting decoys in a manner that requires ducks to fly over a point or other dry ground in order to land in the blocks. Ducks decoy much better if they can come in over water.

LOCATE downed birds by taking directions from another hunter. For instance, a hunter in the blind can keep his eye on the spot where the bird fell and give hand signals to another hunter looking for the bird.

NEOPRENE DOG VESTS will help keep your retriever warm during the late season when the water temperature in near freezing.

TEAMWORK helps set and pick up decoys quickly. While one hunter is running the motor, for example, another is picking up the decoys and a third is wrapping cords and bagging the decoys.

PICK up individual decoys easily using a pole with a hook on the end. This way, you can hook the string at a distance and bring the decoy into the boat.

Field Hunting

If you've ever seen a "swarm" of thousands of mallards descending on a harvested grain field, it's easy to understand why field hunting can be so productive. But even though it affords a great opportunity for taking many kinds of puddle ducks, it is practiced by relatively few hunters, probably because most people associate duck hunting with water. Besides mallards, other ducks commonly taken while field hunting include pintails, wigeon, wood ducks and teal; the latter species does not decoy as well, but they will come in to take a look, offering hunters a good shot.

Ducks often fly out to feed in grain fields in early morning, so it's important to be set up well before the birds arrive. You don't want to be setting out decoys when the ducks are trying to come in. In most cases, the birds fly out to the fields again in late afternoon. Sometimes they stay until after dark, especially on clear nights with a full moon.

As in most other types of duck hunting, you must do some scouting in advance of your hunt. It's hard to predict which field the ducks want to feed in; the best way to determine where and when they're feeding is to drive around and look for milling flocks. If you see flock after flock circling over the same field, you can bet there are plenty of birds on the ground feeding.

Note the time you see the birds, and try to find a landmark that will help you set up in the exact spot when you return to hunt. If you're scouting during the morning feeding period, come back to hunt in the evening. If you're scouting in the evening, come back the next morning.

Most field hunters use decoys to draw the ducks into range. Try to set your decoys on a high spot, with the outermost blocks within gun range. Use oversized shells, silhouettes or full-body decoys for good visibility. The decoys should face in different directions for a natural look. Leave one or more openings for birds to land. Openings should be at least 10 yards across so the birds have plenty of room to set down.

Use a combination of duck and goose decoys when both species are present in the area you are hunting. The goose decoys add greatly to the visibility of your spread, serve as "confidence" decoys for the ducks and may bring in geese too.

Ducks can easily see decoys set on a high spot

Field hunters often use more goose decoys than duck decoys (opposite)

Ducks won't see you if you wear camo clothing and don't move

Ducks flying into feeding fields often circle and mill about for long periods before they land, or they may refuse to set down altogether. They will, however, fly over and take a good look at your decoy spread. If you wait for the birds to land, you may not get any shooting.

In many respects, field hunting is very similar to pass-shooting; the types of shots you get are much the same. Consequently, a fairly tight choke and large shot work best. A 12-gauge with a modified choke and size 1 or 2 shot is a good all-around choice.

Wear camouflage clothing designed to blend in with either the color of the field or the decoys. If you are using snow goose decoys as part of your spread, wear white coveralls and hide among them. Most hunters simply wear camouflage clothing and lie flat on the ground when field hunting. Others prefer to hunt in a pit blind or hunker down in a clump of cover.

You're most likely to get a good shot if you position yourself downwind of the decoys. The birds land into the wind, so you'll have a good shot when they pass overhead.

When hunting in a group, the most experienced hunter should decide when to take them. Then, sit up quickly and shoulder your gun. Some hunters can shoot accurately from a sitting position; others feel

Look for fields with plenty of food

more comfortable kneeling. For safety, all hunters in the party should shoot from the same position.

The best fields for this type of hunting are those with the most crop residue. Once the ducks "eat out" a field, they'll move on to a different one.

Before doing any field hunting, become familiar with state and federal laws on baiting. It is illegal to place corn or any other type of bait in a field for the purpose of attracting waterfowl, and it may even be illegal to shoot at birds that have flown across a field baited by someone else. The laws on baiting are confusing, quite complex and subject to local interpretation.

Decoy Spreads for Field Hunting

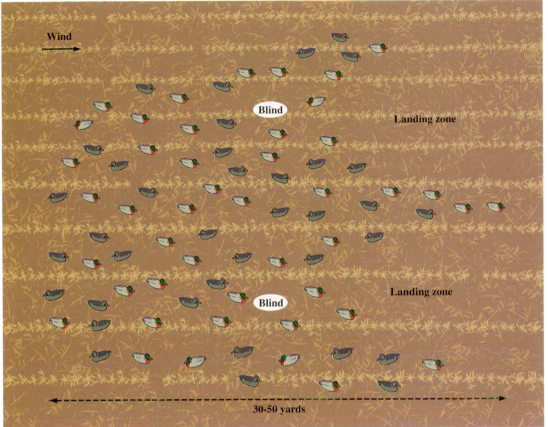

DUCK SPREAD.
Using field or water decoys, make a spread with one or two 10- to 15-yard-wide openings on the downwind side. Wearing camo clothing, lie among the decoys or use a pit blind for cover. The ducks will approach from the downwind side and try to land in the openings.

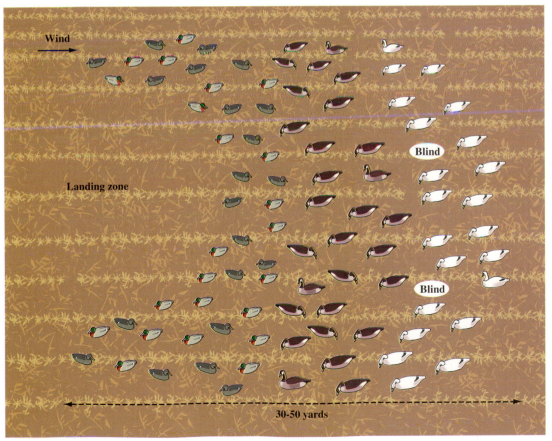

DUCK/GOOSE COMBO SPREAD.
Increase the visibility of your decoy spread by adding some goose decoys. Place either snow or Canada decoys on the downwind side of the spread. On the upwind side, set your duck decoys, leaving a large opening. Even though the birds aren't likely to land there, they will often fly over for a close look. Hide among the goose decoys or in a pit blind near the downwind side of the spread and shoot as the ducks approach.

SET water decoys on high spots so they are more visible. This eliminates the need to buy special field decoys.

USE a goose decoy as a blind when field hunting for ducks. Crawl under a super-magnum shell decoy or lie between two large decoys.

PULL a sheet of camo material over your body to break up your outline when field hunting. This way, you won't have to purchase expensive camo clothing to match the look of the field.

WEAR camo waders to keep dry when hunting muddy fields. Any old waders will do for this type of hunting; it doesn't matter if they leak.

USE a rock pile or other existing cover as a blind. It works well because birds are used to seeing it.

MAKE a dog blind by attaching legs to a large-shell goose decoy. Train your dog to lie down on command and place the decoy over his back.

DIG a depression about 6 inches deep and lie down in it. Cover yourself with cornstalks or stubble. The depression makes you less visible and more comfortable.

CONSTRUCT a "layout board" from a 16-inch-wide by 6-foot-long piece of 5/8- to 3/4-inch plywood. Make a back support on one end from a 2-foot piece of plywood and brace it well. The board keeps you dry while allowing you to sit up and hunt in comfort.

Pass-Shooting Puddlers

In duck-hunting lingo, a pass is a flight corridor that the birds frequently use – for reasons that may not be immediately apparent. Pass-shooting means hunting in such a corridor, without the use of decoys or calls. As the ducks fly by, you simply shoot at the ones within range.

Prehunt scouting is especially critical in pass-shooting, because there is no way to bring the ducks to you. If you're not in precisely the right spot, you'll get no shooting at all.

If possible, do your scouting early or late in the day, when the most ducks are moving. Look for any natural funnels (below) that could concentrate the birds. Avoid hunting near the main duck raft; if the birds do not feel safe when roosting, they will pull out of the area.

Although ducks may use the same flight path for several days, the path may change daily due to variations in wind and weather and shifts in the birds' feeding routine. Try to pattern the birds early in the day and then choose your location accordingly.

Pass-shooters often make the mistake of selecting a spot where the ducks were flying a few days earlier

and staying there, even though no birds come their way. Instead, watch the flight path of the first few flocks that fly out in the morning, then quickly relocate. Chances are, subsequent flocks will follow the same route as the first flocks.

The best time to pass-shoot is in morning or evening, when ducks are most active. But low-pressure systems associated with fronts may keep the birds moving all day. Windy weather also makes for good pass-shooting and keeps the birds flying low.

Many pass-shooters use a full-choke 12-gauge with a 30-inch barrel or buy a 10-gauge, thinking they can shoot ducks at a much greater distance. But long-range shooting greatly increases the crippling rate. Better to use a modified-choke 12-gauge with size 2 to BB loads.

Use the sustained-lead method (p. 56) in most pass-shooting situations. This gives you maximum accuracy when you have enough time to figure your lead and follow the birds, which is normally the case in pass-shooting. The sustained-lead method is especially effective for fast-moving birds at the outer reaches of your range.

Mark downed birds carefully. If you fail to get an accurate mark and swing on another bird, you probably won't be able to find the first one. Take time to line up the downed bird with a distant tree, utility pole, etc., even if it costs you a shot at a second bird.

Natural funnels, such as a cut in the trees, make ideal pass-shooting spots

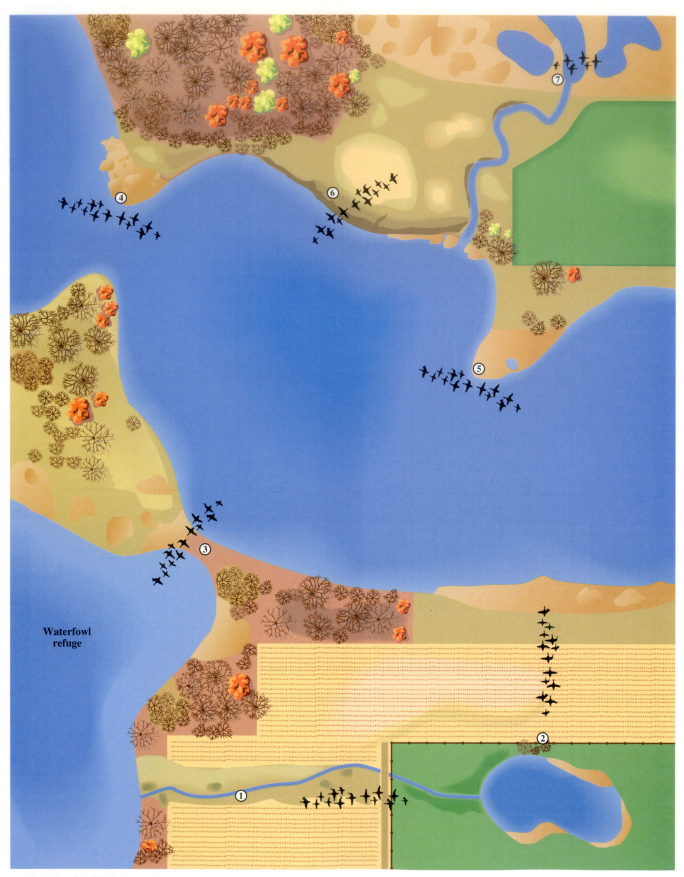

PRIME PASS-SHOOTING LOCATIONS include (1) stream corridors, (2) feeding fields between lakes or potholes, (3) passes between refuges and public waters, (4) narrows between two lake basins, (5) major points, (6) steep hills along the water's edge and (7) emergent vegetation around a cluster of sloughs.

Pass-shooting Tips

PRACTICE shooting at clay targets thrown from all angles to perfect your pass-shooting skills. If you have trouble with a certain shot, that's the one you need to practice the most.

HIDE in creek beds, drainage ditches, weedy fencelines or patches of tall grass when ducks are trading between two fields. Ducks are accustomed to flying over this kind of natural cover.

SET UP a one-man collapsible blind when pass-shooting in areas with sparse cover. When you want to move, simply pick up the blind and carry it to a different spot.

DO NOT shoot at ducks you cannot retrieve. If this bird were to land in the water, the hunter might not be able to reach it by wading.

Jump-Shooting

There are two ways to shoot ducks: wait for them to come to you, or go to them. When the ducks aren't flying or won't respond to your call, the latter option, called *jump-shooting,* is the obvious choice.

Jump-shooting is most productive in bluebird weather, in the middle of the day or anytime the birds are sitting tight. Many waterfowlers hunt over decoys early and late in the day and jump-shoot in midday.

To successfully jump-shoot ducks, there must be enough cover to conceal your approach. If you see a flock of ducks in the middle of a flat field with no vegetation or variation in the terrain for concealment, attempting to sneak up on them is a waste of time.

When you see ducks from a distance, plan a route that will keep you out of their field of vision. Use any available cover between you and the ducks and stay at the lowest possible elevation, if you can. You may be able to walk through a field ditch, but you'll probably have to belly-crawl across a high spot to get close enough for a shot.

But jump-shooting doesn't necessarily require that you first spot the birds and then attempt to sneak up on them. If you suspect that ducks are using an area, but you can't actually see them, try making a blind sneak. This technique is most effective in spots where you've commonly seen ducks before.

Some hunters have a jump-shooting "milk-run" (p. 120), a series of sloughs, creeks, potholes, stock ponds, etc., that they can cover in an hour or two. Ideally, you can establish a circular route that leads back to your starting point.

Always try to keep the wind in your back when jump-shooting on a good-sized body of water, because ducks usually rest on the lee side. Ducks rely mainly on sight and hearing to detect danger, so if you're quiet and stay hidden, they won't know you're coming.

A lightweight 12-gauge shotgun with a modified choke is ideal for jump-shooting. Not only is a light gun easy to carry long distances, it shoulders more quickly for the snap shots that are often required. Because most shots are at close range, use size 1 to 3 shot.

How to Use Different Types of Cover

HIGH SPOTS, such as the dike of a stock dam, make it possible to approach the birds undetected and then rush them for an easy shot.

TALL VEGETATION along the water's edge enables you to stay hidden from the ducks until you're within easy shooting range.

SHORT VEGETATION may be the only cover available. You'll have to crawl on your knees or even belly-crawl to stay concealed.

How to Set Up a "Milk Run" for Jump-shooting

PLAN a milk run that will take you to several good jump-shooting locations and return you to your starting point without backtracking. In this example, the hunter parks on a gravel road and (1) walks into a small pothole near a grain field. From there, he (2) follows the course of a winding stream, (3) checks a small connecting slough, (4) moves on to a shallow marshy area and (5) sneaks up on a stock tank where ducks were spotted from a distance. Then, he returns to the starting point.

How to Spot and Stalk Ducks

SPOT DUCKS from a distance (red line), and plan an approach that will prevent them from seeing you. Look for (1) depressions, such as a creek bottom or ditch, that will allow you to stay low. When you have to cross high ground, use a (2) rock pile or hill for concealment. When you (3) run out of cover, you may have to belly-crawl to reach (4) cover such as cattails or trees that will enable you to walk up on the ducks for a close shot.

Tips for Jump-shooting

CRAWL up on ducks in coverless terrain by holding a bush in front of you. Ducks in open country are accustomed to seeing tumbleweed and other kinds of wind-blown vegetation, so the movement doesn't bother them.

USE a float tube to retrieve ducks you could not reach with waders. Tubes also work well for sneaking up on ducks nestled in deep weeds or other areas that would be difficult to reach by boat.

SNEAK UP on ducks in heavily vegetated marshes using a poke boat or canoe propelled by a push pole. With their tapered shape, they slide through weeds easily and silently. They are also useful for retrieving birds.

SHOOT at ducks the moment they spring from the water, in order to get a head shot. Normally, they'll take off into the wind, then turn and go with it. If you wait too long, you'll have only a long-range tail shot, which is rarely lethal.

FLUSH a large flock of ducks you have snuck up on, rather than shoot at them. The birds will usually trickle back in small groups.

Hunting in Flooded Timber

A flock of mallards that suddenly dive bombs through a small opening in the trees offers a challenge to even the most proficient wingshot.

When you're hunting in a forest of flooded timber, you don't have the luxury of seeing the birds approach from a distance, so there's not much time to prepare for the shot. Sometimes the ducks swoop through the opening before the hunter even has a chance to lift his gun. Consequently, you must be extra alert and have your gun ready at all times.

Mallards and wood ducks feel at home in flooded timber and seek it out during the fall migration. Black ducks, wigeon, gadwall, teal and even ring-necks may also be found in flooded timber. Huge concentrations of ducks winter in flooded timber in the South, particularly in Arkansas, Mississippi, Tennessee and Louisiana.

Flooded timber is most commonly found in river backwaters and man-made lakes. But it is also present in some natural lakes where rising water tables have flooded adjacent timberland. Most ducks prefer flooded timber with water only a foot or two deep. There should be enough open pockets for the birds to land, and the foliage, if any, should not be so dense as to hamper the hunter's visibility.

As in most kinds of duck hunting, scouting is of utmost importance. You need to set up in a spot the ducks have been using, not in a spot you think looks good. Even in a stand of timber that looks the same throughout, the ducks usually return to a spot that has offered them safe refuge in the past.

You may have to walk far back into the trees to reach the right location. Should you get there and find that the ducks are landing elsewhere, pick up and head for that spot.

The timber makes good cover, so a blind is usually unnecessary. Just hide behind a large tree, or sit in the tree's crotch. If the water is too deep for wading, you may need some type of boat blind (pp. 64-67).

Decoys are not really necessary, because they're difficult for the ducks to see among the trees. But a few blocks may encourage the ducks to land once they've flown into a pocket. Set the decoys where they will be most visible and are not hidden by the trees.

Calling may help attract the ducks, but be sure to call cautiously at first and see how the birds react. Vary the volume and calling frequency until you get the ducks' attention. The most common mistake is overcalling or calling too loudly. The noise echoes off the trees and often spooks the birds, causing them to flare or land out of gun range. Cut back on the volume and use a soft-tone call. Sometimes it's best not to call at all.

Because this type of hunting often involves snap shooting at close range, a 12-gauge shotgun with a modified or improved-cylinder choke is the best choice. Most hunters prefer size 3 or 4 steel shot.

It's best to shoot at the ducks as they rise to fly out of the timber, not as they drop in; most hunters find it difficult to lead a descending bird. Hunters sometime let the birds land, then scare them up to get rising shots.

When you down a duck in the timber, be sure to finish it off quickly with a slapper load. Otherwise, it will swim off and soon disappear in the maze of flooded trees.

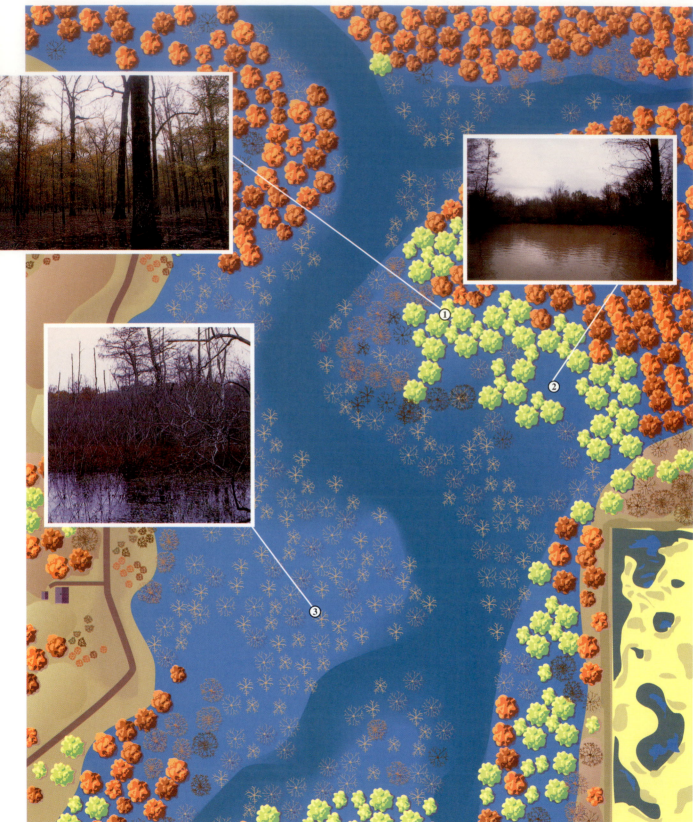

LOOK for (1) green timber, especially when you're hunting mallards or wood ducks. Green foliage usually means the trees are seasonally flooded, so the water they're in is probably shallow. Ducks prefer (2) openings in the timber because they can take off and land more easily. They are reluctant to set down in dense timber with no openings. In (3) dead timber, there is enough open water to attract wigeon, gadwall, wood ducks and, sometimes, divers.

Tips for Hunting in Flooded Timber

USE a "shaker" decoy to create ripples. One shaker in your decoy set is enough to create the illusion that all of the ducks are moving around and tipping up to feed. If you don't have a motorized shaker decoy, manually manipulate a standard decoy using the motion-decoy technique on page 106.

MAKE ripples that imitate those made by ducks. Try splashing with your boot or, if you have a boat, running an electric trolling motor.

CARRY a handheld GPS or a compass when hunting in vast stands of timber. The trees all look the same, so it's easy to get disoriented. With a GPS, be sure to enter a waypoint at the access area.

WEAR Mossy Oak® or Realtree® camouflage when hunting in timber. The patterns and colors of these materials blend in best with the standing trees.

SET UP a portable tree stand for your dog to sit on; otherwise it would have to stand in cold water. These stands help hide the dog, as well. A dog can also sit on a stump, muskrat house or any exposed land.

Float-Hunting

Float-hunting may well be the most overlooked duck-hunting method, but under the right circumstances, it can be one of the most effective. The basic strategy is to use a small boat to float down a stream, surprising ducks resting in slack-water pockets.

The technique works best in midday, when most ducks have finished feeding and are seeking safe refuge. If a stream is float-hunted too often, the ducks will go elsewhere.

You can float-hunt most anytime, but the method works especially well toward season's end. When most potholes and small lakes have frozen up, streams may be the only open water available to the birds.

A winding stream is the best choice for float-hunting. Ducks usually rest in the slack water below the points, making it possible for hunters to float within easy gun range without being seen. On a straight or channelized stream, there is little slack water, and the birds can see you coming from blocks away.

Mallards and wood ducks make up the majority of the float-hunter's bag, but there's a chance of taking any kind of puddle duck. Ringnecks and other divers are a possibility on some larger streams.

Because float-hunting often puts you within a short distance of the ducks, you don't need a tight choke. In most cases, a 12-gauge with an improved-cylinder or modified choke, along with size 2 to 4 steel shot, will do the job.

The ideal float-hunting boat is stable, maneuverable and light enough to haul on a cartop rack. A 14-foot aluminum jon boat is an excellent choice, but it should be controlled with paddles rather than oars, because oarlocks are too noisy. An extra-wide canoe also works well, but a standard-width canoe is too tippy.

Attach a small blind, such as some grass woven into a piece of chicken wire, to the front of your boat. If you point the bow right at the ducks, you can float up on them undetected.

Other than a boat and some warm, water-repellent clothing, float-hunting requires little specialized equipment. You don't need decoys, blinds or calls, and in most instances, it's better to leave your dog at home. A retriever leaping out of a small boat could put you in the water. To be on the safe side, dog or no dog, always wear a camouflage life preserver.

How to Float-hunt for Puddle Ducks

DROP off your boat (1) at the upper end of the reach to be float-hunted. Drop off a second vehicle at the lower end, then drive back to begin your float. (2) Position the shooter in the front of the boat and the paddler in the rear. This way, the shooter does not discharge his gun over the paddler's head. Always remain seated when shooting. Approach the ducks by (3) hugging the inside turns as long as possible (dotted lines). Ducks usually rest below the points, and they won't see you coming until the last minute. When float-hunting by (4) an island, hug the upstream end closely to remain concealed from ducks that are likely to be holding on the downstream side. When hunting (5) backwaters or (6) beaver ponds, beach the boat and make a ground sneak.

Diver Hunting

If you're looking for a wingshooting challenge, diving ducks are the perfect quarry. When a flock of divers streaks along a decoy line, it's not uncommon for a hunter to shoot at the lead bird and drop the third or fourth one back.

Due to the divers' preference for big water, hunters need more and different equipment than they ordinarily do for puddle-duck hunting. Instead of a 12- or 14-foot, shallow-draft duck boat, for instance, you'll need a 16- or 18-foot, deep-hulled semi-V to negotiate water that can turn rough in a hurry. You'll also need more decoys than you would for puddle-duck hunting and, possibly, a floating blind.

The divers' habit of forming large open-water rafts, particularly in late season, adds to the hunting challenge. Some hunters use low-profile sneak or sculling boats to approach birds in open water without alarming them.

Because divers migrate much later in the season than puddle ducks, you'll be hunting in considerably colder weather. Warm, waterproof clothing, including insulated boots and gloves, is a requirement.

Crippled divers often attempt to escape by swimming away underwater or with their head at water level. You'll need a determined, hardy retriever, preferably a Labrador or Chesapeake, that is capable of making long retrieves in cold, choppy water.

In puddle-duck hunting, the idea is to lure birds into the decoys and take them when they're "putting on the brakes," meaning that their wings are cupped and they are about to land. In diver hunting, the birds are less likely to slow down, so you'll probably have to take them as they're winging along a line of decoys that leads to your blind.

Instead of shooting at birds that are barely moving, you're attempting to hit birds barreling along at speeds up to 75 mph. To be successful, you must learn the swing-through technique and do a lot of practicing to determine the proper lead.

Veteran duck hunters will tell you that divers are less intelligent than puddlers. While a puddle duck may circle your decoy spread several times checking for anything that looks suspicious, a diver will usually zoom in close enough for a shot right away.

Calling is seldom necessary in diver hunting. The birds spot the decoys from a distance and their curiosity draws them in without any vocal enticement. Nevertheless, many hunters try calling anyway, using a diver call or rolling their tongue against a mallard call to mimic the characteristic diver "purr."

Divers differ from puddlers in that they do not hesitate to land in rough water. As a result, there is no need to set your decoys off a lee shore. It's more important to set them where the birds are feeding, regardless of wind direction.

Yet another difference: divers do most all of their feeding on the water, so the field-hunting techniques that work so well for puddle ducks are not effective for divers. Practically all diver hunting is done on the water or on passes between two bodies of water.

Diver hunting is not for everyone. Not only does it require a high tolerance for inclement weather, it can be a lot of work. But if you're a hardy soul who loves the whistle of wings, there's no more exciting shooting.

Pass-Shooting for Divers

Pass-shooting for divers is much like pass-shooting for puddlers, with one exception: divers nearly always fly near water, so that's where you must hunt them. Because divers feed, drink and rest on the water, you will seldom find them trading between lakes and feeding fields, as puddlers often do.

Successful pass-shooters know how to find a productive pass. Prime shooting locations (opposite) are determined by scouting the birds' flight patterns and quizzing local hunters about traditional passes.

You can pass-shoot divers most anytime, but hunting is usually best during the migration period, when large numbers of birds move into your area. Most divers migrate several weeks after the heavy puddle-duck migration. Daily movement peaks around sunrise and sunset, especially in calm weather, although divers are more likely to move about in midday than are puddlers. Windy weather or a little rain, sleet or snow often keeps the birds flying all day.

Try to position yourself directly under the flight path most of the birds are using. Once the flight pattern has been established on a given day, the birds tend to stick with it, barring a significant wind or weather change. If you're not within shooting range, it pays to reposition as quickly as possible.

Repositioning is fairly easy when hunting divers, because you don't need as much cover as you would when hunting the warier puddlers. All that's necessary is something like sparse brush to break up your outline. Some hunters wear a camouflage outfit and stand motionless right in the open, using face paint or a face mask to eliminate facial glare. If your face is not covered, resist the urge to look up.

A 10- or 12-gauge shotgun with a modified choke and 28- to 30-inch barrel, along with size 2 to BB steel shot, gives you a tight pattern and good long-range killing power. Try to pick out an individual bird and shoot at it using the sustained-lead method (p. 56). Divers often fly in tight clumps, and hunters commonly make the mistake of flock-shooting.

When pass-shooting, there's always the tendency to "stretch your barrel" in an attempt to bring down high fliers. But at a range of more than 40 yards, you risk crippling a high percentage of the birds you target.

Before shooting at any birds, be sure they will fall in a spot where they can be easily retrieved. If you're hunting in waders, don't shoot at birds that would land in water too deep for wading. In late season, don't target birds that would land on thin ice. Finish off any cripples with a slapper load before they can dive and escape. Be sure a downed bird is dead before swinging on another bird.

SET two or three decoys in front of your hide when pass-shooting. The blocks will often bring the birds in closer, giving you a better shot.

PRIME LOCATIONS for pass-shooting divers include: (1) major points, (2) flooded roadbeds or old railroad crossings, (3) passes between two bodies of water, (4) a narrows between two lakes, (5) long, straight shorelines (on windy days), (6) islands and (7) points on smaller adjacent lakes.

Hunting Divers on Big Water

Hunting divers on big water requires a substantial investment in equipment and a willingness to endure cold, blustery weather that would keep most folks in a cozy chair next to the fireplace. But die-hard big-water hunters are often rewarded with flights of divers numbering in the thousands.

Most divers are late migrants, explaining why hunters may have to contend with sleet, snow, stiff winds and below-freezing temperatures.

Diving ducks prefer the open expanses of natural and man-made lakes, good-sized rivers and coastal bays and estuaries. Large rafts of divers gather on these waters, particularly in late season when smaller lakes are starting to freeze up.

Divers raft up in a certain spot for one reason: food. They may be feeding on a bed of wild celery, a school of small fish or a concentration of larval insects or shellfish. Once they start to feed in a particular area, they will usually continue to do so until the food supply is exhausted or they are driven away by hunting pressure or weather.

The usual strategy is to scout in late afternoon or evening to pinpoint the area in which the ducks are feeding, and then set up in that exact spot early the

Redheads rafting in open water

next morning. If the birds are feeding close to shore, you can set up a blind on land, usually on a long point jutting into open water. Otherwise, you'll need a floating blind, stilt blind, boat blind or some type of low-profile boat.

Where you set your decoys is more important than how many you set. A few dozen decoys set right in the feeding area will draw more birds than a few hundred set a quarter mile away. If you're competing with a nearby hunter, however, and he has more decoys set in an equally good area, he will probably pull more birds than you will. There is no definite rule on how many decoys are needed.

You can increase the drawing power of your decoy spread by using oversized blocks or setting individual blocks farther apart, making the spread look larger. Another good way to draw more divers is by flagging (p. 135).

Calling, on the other hand, is seldom necessary in big-water hunting. The birds rely mainly on their vision to spot rafts of birds from a distance. Some hunters, however, make a diver purr once the birds get close enough to hear it.

Low-profile boats, including layout, sneak and sculling boats (p. 135), have long been popular for hunting sea ducks in open water and are gaining favor on large freshwater lakes. All are towed or carried out to the hunting area with a larger boat and used in conjunction with a good-sized decoy spread.

A 12-gauge semi-automatic or pump with a modified or improved-cylinder choke, along with steel shot in sizes 3 to BB, is ideal for hunting big-water divers. With a double-barrel, you won't have enough shots to finish off cripples, which can easily disappear into open water if not killed right away. Your gun should have a barrel no longer than 28 inches.

This way, when the ducks approach your blind at high speed, then decide to veer one way or the other, you can swing quickly.

Coldwater dogs, primarily Labs and Chesapeakes, are the best choice for this type of hunting. Besides their hardiness, they have great determination – a requirement for the difficult, long-distance retrieves they're often faced with.

Big-water hunting is seldom done in the evening; picking up large numbers of decoys after dark is difficult and sometimes dangerous. And if you run into trouble, there's nobody around to help. Carry a two-way radio, cellular phone or flare gun if you'll be hunting in a remote area.

Warm, water-resistant clothing is a requirement. If you're hunting on water rather than land, you'll need a good-sized, seaworthy boat and life jackets for each hunter. Don't overload your boat with dozens of decoys, anchors and other equipment; tow a smaller boat to carry excess gear. Resist the temptation to hunt in water too rough for your boat – it's not worth risking your life for a duck.

Decoy spreads for big-water divers should lead the birds to within easy shooting distance, but the birds don't necessarily have to land. Some hunters simply set out a straight line of decoys leading into open water, but most use some kind of "J" or "V" formation, as shown on the next page. Others use a double-pod setup similar to that used for puddle ducks. The best decoy spreads have an obvious landing zone.

Because big-water hunters normally use from 50 to more than 200 decoys, setting them can take a long time. To speed up the process, try rigging the decoys on longlines (p. 63). Each longline should hold 12 to 16 decoys spaced 3 to 5 feet apart. The cord should have a 5- to 10-pound anchor on each end.

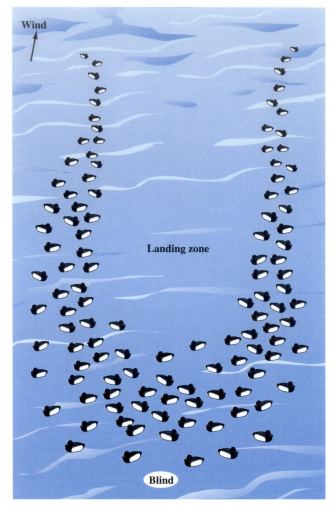

THE J-HOOK. This setup works well off a point or in open water. The long tail extends well beyond shooting range. The outer decoys are spaced farther apart than the inner ones. The largest clump of decoys is placed at the hook of the "J," which forms a landing zone.

THE V-FORMATION. This setup is similar to the J-hook, but it has two tails extending out into the water, rather than one, giving the birds an additional option for approaching the blind. As in the J-hook setup, the outer decoys are spaced farther apart than the inner ones.

DOUBLE-POD. This spread, intended to draw in ducks that want to land, has two large pods of decoys with a good-sized landing area in the middle.

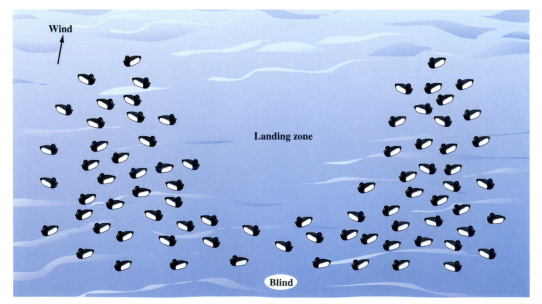

How to Hunt from Low-profile Boats

LAYOUT BOAT. Anchor the boat at the head of the decoy spread. The anchor rope should be attached at the bow and the hunter should sit with the wind at his back. The ducks will land into the wind, so the hunter will be facing them. Some hunters place a few decoys right on the boat to help it blend in with the spread.

SCULLING BOAT. Normally used without decoys, these boats are propelled by a sculling oar that sticks out of a hole in the transom. The skuller maneuvers the boat toward a raft of ducks until he is within shooting range.

Tips for Big-water Divers

WAVE a black flag when you spot distant ducks. The motion resembles other ducks flying or landing. Stop flagging once the ducks start to head your way.

MAKE inexpensive diver decoys by painting black patches on white bleach jugs.

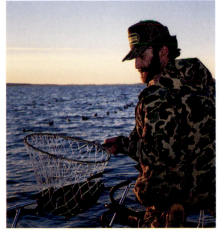

COLLECT downed ducks in rough water by scooping them up with a landing net. This way, you don't have to lean over the boat and risk getting wet.

Hunting Divers on Small Waters

Most waterfowlers associate diver hunting with big water, and, in most cases, that's where you'll find the largest concentrations of birds. But smaller waters offer some excellent diver-hunting opportunities, require substantially less equipment and, because they're overlooked by most diving-duck devotees, allow you to get away from the crowd. Also, the birds can't escape hunting pressure by rafting up out in the middle, as they often do on big water.

Divers prefer small lakes and large potholes with water at least 5 feet deep. Look for them in open water rather than weedy areas; divers avoid the emergent vegetation that is paradise to puddle ducks. You can also find divers on many small- to medium-sized rivers.

Waters used by divers must offer a good supply of food, either submerged plants, crustaceans, aquatic insects, small fish or a combination of the above. Often, you'll see divers consistently using one small lake while avoiding a seemingly similar lake nearby. Chances are, one lake has a good food supply and the other doesn't. The only way to determine the best body of water to hunt and where to hunt it is to spend some time scouting.

Because diving ducks are late migrants and small bodies of water freeze earlier than large ones, the window for hunting small-water divers may be relatively short. After small waters freeze up, the birds congregate on larger bodies of water.

If there are some divers around in early season, they will most likely move early and late in the day. But as the weather gets colder, the birds begin feeding more to fuel their migration, so they spend more of their time moving about. In the latter part of the season, they'll usually move throughout the day, even in bluebird weather.

If you're a small-water puddle-duck hunter, you probably own all the equipment needed for small-water divers. You can use the same boats, blinds, calls and even decoys.

As in big-water diver hunting, flagging helps get the attention of distant birds and draw them toward your decoys. Although calling is seldom necessary, some hunters make a one- to three-note purr to bring the birds in closer. If you're using a combination decoy set that contains puddle-duck or goose decoys, a call that mimics those birds will help gain the divers' confidence.

The divers' high-speed, low-altitude flight requires a gun you can swing rapidly. Most hunters prefer a 12-gauge pump or semi-automatic with a barrel no longer than 28 inches and a modified choke, along with steel shot in sizes 3 to BB. If you prefer to use a double-barrel, always save one shot for finishing off a cripple; otherwise, it may dive and swim away underwater while you're reloading. A cold-hardy retriever, usually a Lab or Chesapeake, will keep bird loss to a minimum.

You don't need a large spread of diver decoys to bring in divers. Many hunters simply use one or two dozen mallard decoys for the main part of their spread, and then string out a few diver decoys to form a tail that will lead the birds to the blind. This combination spread often attracts as many puddlers as divers.

J-HOOK. You can set a J-hook along a straight shoreline, as long as the wind is blowing parallel to shore. The leg of the J should be aligned with the wind, and the pocket of the J, where the birds will usually land, should be directly in front of the blind. With the wind blowing offshore from a point (inset), set a group of decoys just off the tip. Then, run a line of decoys straight out into the lake, forming a short J-hook. Gradually increase the spacing between the blocks as you go out. This spread is similar to the J-hook used for big-water divers, but it is shorter and contains fewer blocks.

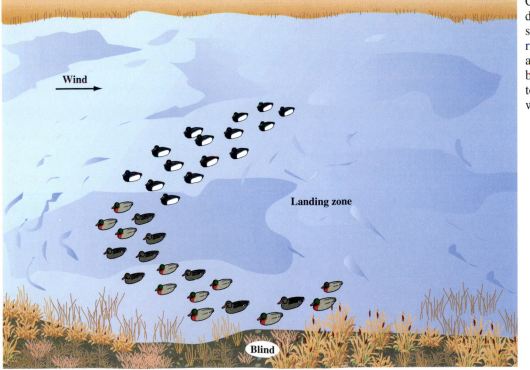

C-SET. Set a "C"-shaped decoy formation in a deep, slow-moving pool of a river. The wind should be at the back of the C. The blind should be adjacent to the opening of the C, where the ducks will land.

Hunting Sea Ducks

Sea-duck hunting is a sport for the most dedicated of waterfowlers. Hunters may have to endure lengthy boat rides in 8-foot waves and near-zero-degree temperatures. But they're often rewarded by seeing tremendous flocks of ducks.

The best time to hunt sea duck is in early morning, when ducks rafting in open water fly near the coast to feed on snails, small mollusks and crustaceans.

Always hunt between roosting and feeding areas. If you hunt right in the roosting or feeding area, the birds will probably move to a different location.

The most effective method is to hunt from a boat on open water, because you can get close to the feeding area. But you can also pass-shoot or set decoys off points or shorelines near the feeding area.

Decoying works best on calm, sunny days. Because sea ducks fly only a few feet above the water, they may have a hard time seeing your decoys in cloudy, windy weather.

You may have to set decoys in water 40 to 50 feet deep, so longlines (p. 63) are recommended. Sea-duck hunters often use lines well over 100 feet long. A minimum of 60 blocks is needed to get the birds' attention.

A 12-gauge semi-automatic or pump with a modified choke, along with steel shot in sizes 2 to BB, is necessary for these large, heavily insulated ducks. Always try to save your third shot for quickly finishing off cripples; otherwise, they may dive and show up hundreds of yards away.

Gear for Sea-duck Hunting

TENDING BOATS are often needed to haul smaller boats, hunters and equipment.

CAMOUFLAGE COVERS are used to make hunting boats resemble rock piles or dark-colored water.

Wind

Landing zone

Blind

SEA-DUCK SPREAD. Attach a 5- to 10-pound anchor to the upwind end of each longline. Run lines on either side of the blind, leaving a 10- to 15-yard opening in the middle for a landing zone.

How to Make and Use Silhouette Decoy Sleds

Making a Silhouette Sled
Materials:
- 1 - 1" x 4" x 14" pine board.
- 1 - 1" x 4" x 18" pine board.
- 2 - 1/8" plywood or Masonite® silhouette cutouts of desired species.
- 8 - 1 1/2" Sheetrock® screws.
- 1 - 1 1/2" x 1/4" eyebolt.

18"

14"

24"

USE silhouette sleds, which can be neatly stacked so they take up less space than ordinary decoys. Attach the sleds to longlines; each should be rigged with about 12 sleds. Tie a full-body floating decoy to each end of the line to help keep the silhouettes afloat in rough water.

CARRY silhouette sleds by stacking one on top of the other as shown. The tapered design makes stacking possible.

Index

Contributing Photographers (Note: T=Top, C=Center, B=Bottom, L=Left, R=Right, I=Inset)

Aigrette Photography
Coos Bay, Oregon
©*Steve Holt p. 47BRI*

Cliff Beittel
York, Pennsylvania
©*Cliff Beittel p. 42T, 42I*

Black Hawk Productions
Mechanicsville, Virginia
©*Dwight Dyke p. 66CL*

Denver Bryan
Bozeman, Montana
©*Denver Bryan pp. 21T, 77BL*

Bruce "Wicker Bill" Crist
Ft. Pierre, South Dakota
©*Bruce Crist p. 9CR*

Dembinsky & Associates
Owosso, Michigan
©*Barbara Gerlach p. 33I*
©*Gary Meszaros pp. 11BL, 19B, 92T*
©*Skip Moody p. 13BR*
©*Stan Osolinski p. 28L*
©*Rod Planck p. 45T*
©*Gisjbert Van Frankenhuszen p. 121BL*

Jeanne Drake
Las Vegas, Nevada
©*Jeanne Drake pp. 30-31T, 68-69T*

FRS Photography
Bellingham, Washington
©*Fredrick Sears pp. 21TI, 32T, 35T, 35TI, 38TI, 46T, 47BR*

Mike Gnatowski
Ludington, Michigan
©*Mike Gnatowski pp. 75T, 135T*

The Green Agency
Belgrade, Montana
©*Bill Buckley p. 93TR*
©*Rich Kirchner p. 39TR, 39TRI*
©*Dale Spartas p. 117BR*

Cathy & Gordon Illg
Lakewood, Colorado
©*Cathy & Gordon Illg pp. 26B, 27T, 27TI, 33T, 34B, 34BI, 39BR, 40BI*

Mark Kayser
Ft. Pierre, South Dakota
©*Mark Kayser pp. 118-119T*

Gary Kramer
Willows, California
©*Gary Kramer pp. 9CL, 11BC, 17CL, 23T, 43T, 67C, 139TL*

Lance Krueger
McAllen, Texas
©*Lance Krueger p. 76BI*

Tim Leary
Franconia, New Hampshire
©*Tim Leary pp. 8, 9BC, 11TL, 75B, 76TI, 138, 139CL, 139BL, 139BR*

Gerard Lemmo
Glen Falls, New York
©*Gerard Lemmo pp. 12B, 19I*

Stephanie McCloskey
Oakland, California
©*Stephanie McCloskey p. 47TI*

Bill Marchel
Fort Ripley, Minnesota
©*Bill Marchel pp. 6-7, 10T, 10BR, 17TR, 17CR, 18T, 18TI, 22, 24L, 24I, 25I, 31BR, 36B, 38T, 41TI, 57TR, 66BR, 72C, 77BC, 77BR, 93BR, 121TR, 136T*

Maslowski Wildlife Productions
Cincinnati, Ohio
©*Dave Maslowski p. 43TI*

Margaret Thompson Mathewson
Amity, Oregon
©*Margaret Thompson Mathewson p. 135C, 135BL*

Minden Pictures
Aptos, California
©*Jim Brandenburg p. 9T*

Neal Mishler
Great Falls, Montana
©*Neal Mishler, duck images on cover*

Scott Nielsen
Superior, Wisconsin
©*Scott Nielsen pp. 11BR, 12BI, 13CL, 13CR, 16, 30BL, 30BR, 31BL, 32TI, 37B, 41TR*

Rich Images
Morro Bay, California
©*Richard Hansen pp. 12CR, 20I, 41BR, 46I, 47TR*

Dick Simpson
Madison, South Dakota
©*Dick Simpson pp. 73B, 106BL*

Dale Spartas
Bozeman, Montana
©*Dale Spartas pp. 67BL, 67BR, 93TL, 107TR*

Ron Spomer
Troy, Idaho
©*Ron Spomer pp. 10BL, 39BRI, 128-129*

Texas Inprint
Dallas, Texas
©*David Sams p. 133*

Vireo
Philadelphia, Pennsylvania
©*Rob Curtis p. 45TI*
©*A. & E. Morris p. 29*

Keith Walters
Bozeman, Maryland
©*Keith Walters p. 135BR*

The Wildlife Collection
Brooklyn Heights, New York
©*D. Robert Franz pp. 40B, 130*
©*Martin Harvey p. 41BI*
©*Robert Lankinen p. 44*
©*Tom Vezo pp. 20B, 23TI, 25T, 26BI*

Wildlife Research Photography
Mammoth Lakes, California
©*Moose Peterson pp. 9BL, 10BC*

Matt Young
Memphis, Tennessee
©*Matt Young p. 75C*

Gary Zahm
Los Banos, California
©*Gary Zahm pp. 4-5, 11CR, 12T, 13BL, 14, 17B, 37BI, 57C, 57BL, 57BR, 121BR*

Contributing Manufacturers

Exclusive Supplier
Herter's
P.O. Box 1819
Burnsville, Minnesota 55337
1-800-654-3825

Action Decoys
P.O. Box 3336
Palestine, Texas 75802

Alumacraft Boats
315 W. St. Julien
St. Peter, Minnesota 83638

Browning
One Browning Place
Morgan, Utah 84050

Cabela's, Inc.
812 13th Avenue
Sidney, Nebraska 69160

Carlson Championship Calls
12200 College Street RR 2
Cedar Rapids, Iowa 52404

Carry-Lite Decoys, Inc.
5203 W. Clinton Avenue
Milwaukee, Wisconsin 53223-4781

Columbia Sportswear
P.O. Box 83239
Portland, Oregon 972383

Duck Commander Co.
538 Mouth of Cypress Road
West Monroe, Louisiana 71292

Feather-Flex Decoys
1655 Swan Lake Road
Bossier City, Louisiana 71111

Federal Cartridge Co.
900 Ehlen Drive
Anoka, Minnesota 55303

Flagman Products
1225 West Center Street
Oronoco, Minnesota 55303

Flambeau Products
15981 Valplast Road
P.O. Box 97
Middlefield, Ohio 44062

Force Fin
715 Kimball Avenue
Santa Barbara, California 93103

Haas Outdoors
101 East Main
West Point, Mississippi 39973

Haydel's Game Calls, Inc.
5018 Hazel Jones Road
Bossier City, Louisiana 71111

Hobie Outback
502 N. Third Street, Suite 202
McCall, Idaho 83638

I.W.S.
P.O. Box 30
Madison, Nebraska 68748

Kobuk
2639 N. Grand Avenue #268
Santa Ana, California 92705

Lohman Game Calls
P.O. Box 220
Neosho, Missouri 64850

Mallard Master
Box 291, Dept. 22
Jonesville, Louisana 71343

Mossy Oak
P.O. Box 757
West Point, Mississippi 39773

Outlaw Decoys, Inc.
10907 E. Marietta
STE 2
Spokane, Washington 99206

Rich-N-Tone Products
348 Byhalia Road
Collierville, Tennessee 38017

Riverside Products, Inc.
P.O. Box 1331
Pine Bluff, Arkansas 71613-1331

Stearns Manufacturing Company
P.O. Box 1498
St. Cloud, Minnesota 56302

Top Line Manufacturing
901 Murray Road
East Hanover, New Jersey 07936

W.C. Russell Moccasin Co.
285 S.W. Franklin
Berlin, Wisconsin 54923

Woods Calls Inc.
P.O. Box 29434
Lincoln, Nebraska 68529

The Hunting & Fishing Library® is the most complete source of How-To Information for the Outdoorsman

The Complete Hunter™ Series

• *The Art of Hunting • White-tailed Deer*
• *Dressing & Cooking Wild Game*
• *America's Favorite Wild Game Recipes*
• *Upland Game Birds • Wild Turkey*
• *Advanced Whitetail Hunting*
• *North American Game Birds*
• *North American Game Animals*
• *Bowhunting Equipment & Skills*
• *Understanding Whitetails*
• *Muzzleloading • Duck Hunting*
• *Venison Cookery (8/97)*
• *Game Bird Cookery (10/97)*

The Freshwater Angler™ Series

• *The Art of Fly Tying • Largemouth Bass*
• *Fishing With Artificial Lures • Trout*
• *The Art of Freshwater Fishing*
• *America's Favorite Fish Recipes*
• *Panfish • Fishing Tips & Tricks*
• *Cleaning & Cooking Fish*
• *Secrets of the Fishing Pros*
• *Smallmouth Bass • Walleye*
• *Fishing Rivers & Streams*
• *Fishing With Live Bait*
• *Advanced Bass Fishing*
• *Northern Pike & Muskie*
• *Freshwater Gamefish of North America*

The Complete FLY FISHERMAN™ Series

• *Fly-Tying Techniques & Patterns*
• *Fly Fishing for Trout in Streams–
  Subsurface Techniques*
• *Fly-Fishing Equipment & Skills*
• *The Art of Fly Tying CD-ROM*
• *Fly Rod Gamefish–
  The Freshwater Species*

For a list of participating retailers near you, call 1-800-328-0590